IRISH SHORTS

Two-handers from the Abbey Theatre, Ireland

IRISH SHORTS

GARY DUGGAN ▪ STOP/OVER

STACEY GREGG ▪ WHEN COWS GO BOOM

NANCY HARRIS ▪ LOVE IN A GLASS JAR

ROSEMARY JENKINSON ▪ MEETING MISS IRELAND

DEIRDRE KINAHAN ▪ SALAD DAY

LISA McGEE ▪ NINETEEN NINETY-TWO

PHILLIP McMAHON ▪ INVESTMENT POTENTIAL

ELAINE MURPHY ▪ RIBBONS

Selected and introduced by Aideen Howard

NICK HERN BOOKS
London
www.nickhernbooks.co.uk

A Nick Hern Book

Irish Shorts first published in Great Britain in 2013 as a paperback original by Nick Hern Books Limited, The Glasshouse, 49a Goldhawk Road, London W12 8QP, in association with the Abbey Theatre, Ireland

Stop/Over copyright © 2013 Gary Duggan
When Cows Go Boom copyright © 2013 Stacey Gregg
Love in a Glass Jar copyright © 2013 Nancy Harris
Meeting Miss Ireland copyright © 2013 Rosemary Jenkinson
Salad Day copyright © 2013 Deirdre Kinahan
Nineteen Ninety-Two copyright © 2013 Lisa McGee
Investment Potential copyright © 2013 Phillip McMahon
Ribbons copyright © 2013 Elaine Murphy
Introduction copyright © 2013 Aideen Howard

Cover design: Nick Hern Books, London
Cover image: The Ha'penny Bridge, Dublin © Patryk Kosmider/www.shutterstock.com

Typeset by Nick Hern Books, London
Printed in Great Britain by CPI Group (UK) Ltd

A CIP catalogue record for this book is available from the British Library

ISBN 978 1 84842 317 6

Contents

Introduction

In late 2007 the Abbey Theatre commissioned six up-and-coming playwrights to write a short play for two characters. The plays were to be twenty minutes long and would be presented as public readings. Inspired by *Romeo and Juliet*, then running on the Abbey stage, and by Sam Shepard's *Fool for Love* on the Peacock stage, the short plays would be presented as 20:Love.

We thought to introduce new voices to the Abbey Theatre, to welcome playwrights at or near the beginning of their careers, and to work with them to develop and present a new short play without the pressures and scrutiny that go with a full production at Ireland's National Theatre. My wish, too, was that the commission would begin a long working relationship with a new generation of writers.

Of course, the Abbey has a fine tradition of short plays. When the theatre first opened its doors on 27th December 1904, it was with a triple bill. Indeed, for many years later the short works of Lady Gregory, William Butler Yeats and John Millington Synge were central to the Abbey repertoire. In the 1950s, Ernest Blythe introduced the one-act play in Irish after the main billing. Elsewhere, Samuel Beckett too made frequent use of the short-play form to different ends.

For the purposes of writer development, the short play presents distinct advantages. For the playwright who has only written monologues, it poses the challenge of dialogue without the burden of sustaining plot. For the writer disenchanted by structural constraints, it offers a reprieve from the long form. For those who start with ideas, it's a perfect structure in which to introduce an incendiary notion and play out its consequences over twenty minutes. In addition, by commissioning six writers and by presenting a number of plays together, we hoped to overhear the dialogues of a young generation.

Since then the short-play commissions have become an annual event, and we have commissioned nineteen short plays in English, and three in Irish, by some of the most exciting playwrights in Ireland, making for a significant repertoire of short plays which have been seen and heard by more than 1,300 people. This volume contains only eight of those plays – by Nancy Harris, Stacey Gregg, Phillip McMahon, Gary Duggan, Rosemary Jenkinson, Deirdre Kinahan, Lisa McGee and Elaine Murphy. In each case, the play was that writer's first for the Abbey Theatre, and the intention behind this collection is therefore to promote their early work and extend its life beyond the first outing in the Peacock.

Sometimes the plays prefigure concerns that appear in later work. *Love in a Glass Jar* by Nancy Harris subverts the conventions of bedroom drama to make for a witty, thoughtful play about IVF, DIY-style. When Eve meets Patrick in the bedroom of a hotel about 'an hour outside Dublin', she's completing a transaction which has begun on the internet. These two strangers, who have 'met' and corresponded online, together face the inconvenient truth that – despite the elaborate arrangements that have set it in motion – this first and only meeting is an essential part of the deal of procreation! Nancy's later play, *No Romance*, produced in 2011, also explores – among other things – the role that technology plays in our romantic imaginations and our acting-out of relationships.

Gary Duggan's *Stop/Over* self-consciously uses the short form to stage a stopover in New York on the journey from California back home to Dublin. In the thirty-one hours between arrival at JFK and departure from Newark, former lovers F and M spend a day and night on the town. When M says, 'The trouble with Dublin, with Ireland, is you can't move without bumping into someone you know', he could be describing the dramatic structure of Gary's later play, *Shibari*, produced on the Peacock stage in 2012.

One of the delights of multiple commissions from the same starting point is in the diversity of dramas that emerge. Audiences coming to the theatre on a single evening will see a range of responses, deviations, evasions and variations on a theme. *When Cows Go Boom* by Stacey Gregg is an oblique parable of love set against the backdrop of an imaginary landscape.

By contrast, when Phillip McMahon took on the commission to write his first dialogue play he made cheeky, direct reference to the Shakespeare play that was running at the same time as his. *Investment Potential* makes clever use of the tight form to present glimpses of the middle, beginning and end of a relationship. 'Two houses both alike in investment potential… and we're still renting.'

Like Phillip, Elaine Murphy also wrote her first dialogue play in response to The Fairer Sex commission in 2009. It is, I believe, the first appearance of gender reassignment surgery in a new play at the Abbey Theatre. *Ribbons* was perhaps the prettiest title of the season, but the play offers a thoughtful and wholly unsentimental glimpse of a relationship which is about to be transformed for ever.

When we meet Rosemary Jenkinson's sister and brother Kathy and Stevie Ireland, it's on the eve of a speed-dating event in Belfast. Their hilarious rehearsal of tactical speed-dating is written with characteristic brio, but the linguistic energy of *Meeting Miss Ireland* is deceptive too, barely disguising the pathological relationship at the heart of the play.

A quieter, more sinister energy is at play in *Nineteen Ninety-Two* by Lisa McGee, in which she explores the consequences of a child murder by an older girl.

Deirdre Kinahan's real-time portrayal of the loneliness of life in an old folks' home in *Salad Day* is the only play in this selection to write characters in older age. In the speeches and the silences that fill the play is a subtle depiction of character in an unfamiliar, inhospitable environment. Deirdre later rewrote and expanded this play to become *Halcyon Days*, which was produced by her own company Tall Tales at the Dublin Theatre Festival in 2012.

When I thought of publishing these plays, my first port of call was Nick Hern at Nick Hern Books, whose commitment to new

writing for the stage is unequalled. Together, we have had the
happiest of collaborations. My frustration at only being able to
include eight plays is allayed a little by the hope that this
volume will encourage future productions and that this, in turn,
will make an argument for putting together a second volume of
the wonderful later plays.

Aideen Howard
Literary Director

AIDEEN HOWARD

Aideen Howard is the Literary Director of the Abbey Theatre
with responsibility for commissioning new plays and
developing new writers for both stages of the Abbey Theatre.
She set up the Abbey Theatre's New Playwrights Programme in
2009. Aideen holds an MA in Drama from UCD and a BA in
English and German from Trinity College, Dublin. She was the
first Artistic Director of Mermaid Arts Centre where she
programmed and ran a multidisciplinary arts venue. She has
also worked as literary consultant to Arts Council projects and
previously as dramaturg at the Abbey Theatre.

The Abbey Theatre is Ireland's national theatre. It was founded by W.B. Yeats and Lady Augusta Gregory. Since it first opened its doors in 1904, the theatre has played a vital and often controversial role in the literary, social and cultural life of Ireland.

The Abbey produces an annual programme of diverse, engaging, innovative Irish and international theatre and invests in and promotes new Irish writers and artists. We do this by placing the writer and theatre-maker at the heart of all that we do, commissioning and producing exciting new work and creating discourse and debate on the political, cultural and social issues of the day. Our aim is to present great theatre art in a national context so that the stories told on stage have a resonance with artists and audiences alike.

Over the years, the Abbey Theatre has nurtured and premiered the work of major playwrights such as J.M. Synge and Sean O'Casey as well as contemporary classics from the likes of Sebastian Barry, Marina Carr, Bernard Farrell, Brian Friel, Frank McGuinness, Thomas Kilroy, Tom Mac Intyre, Tom Murphy, Mark O'Rowe, Billy Roche and Sam Shepard.

We also support the new generation of Irish writers at the Abbey Theatre including Carmel Winters, Nancy Harris, Elaine Murphy, Stacey Gregg, Gary Duggan and Phillip McMahon.

Abbey Theatre Board of Directors
Dr. Bryan McMahon (Chairman), Jane Brennan, Paul Davis, Moya Doherty, John Finnegan, Róise Goan, Thomas Kilroy, James McNally, Mark Ryan.

Abbey Theatre Senior Management Team
Fiach Mac Conghail (Director/CEO), Declan Cantwell (Director of Finance and Administration), Oonagh Desire (Director of Public Affairs and Development), Gavin Harding (Technical Director), Aideen Howard (Literary Director).

STOP/OVER

Gary Duggan

GARY DUGGAN

Shibari, Gary Duggan's first full-length play to be staged at the Abbey Theatre, premiered on the Peacock stage as part of the 2012 Dublin Theatre Festival. *Stop/Over,* his short-play commission, was presented on the Peacock stage as part of the 20:Love series of public readings in 2008. In 2006, Gary won the Stewart Parker Trust Award for his first play, *Monged* (Fishamble: The New Play Company, also Belgrade Theatre, Coventry). His other work includes *Dedalus Lounge* (Pageant Wagon, also Royal Family Productions, New York); *Mission* (part of an anthology show End of Lines, Origin Theatre Company, New York); *Trans-Euro Express* (Pageant Wagon, also Fundamental Theater Project and Irish Arts Center, New York) and *Neuropolis* (Duggan & Logue, ABSOLUT Fringe). *Monged* and *Dedalus Lounge* have been translated into Romanian and have performed in repertory in Bucharest. Gary has collaborated with director Louise Lowe on two shows, *Rockpaperscissors* and *Basin* (ABSOLUT Fringe). Gary also writes for film and television. He created and wrote three episodes (directing one) of *Happyslapper*, a web drama for RTÉ's first Storyland series, and has co-written (with Rob Cawley) *Amber*, a four-part drama for RTÉ.

Stop/Over was first performed as a rehearsed reading as part of the 20:Love play-reading series for the Abbey Theatre, Dublin, in 2008. The cast was as follows:

M	Paul Reid
F	Lisa Lambe
Director	Rachel West

An expanded version of *Stop/Over* was later performed at Solstice as part of the Cork Midsummer Festival in June 2011, with the following cast:

M	Sam Peter Corry
F	Aoibhin Garrihy
Director	Gavin Logue

Characters

M, *twenties*
F, *twenties*

Going Back

F. This is now and then.

M. This is our place.

F. This is New York.

M. This is almost ten years ago.

F. Is it?

M. It is.

F. Jesus.

M. When you were young and your heart was an open book.

F. You used to say…

M. I used to say…?

Reacquainting

M. You look the same.

F. I do? Same as when?

M. Then. Last time I saw you.

F. Not older?

M. No. You haven't changed.

F. I never change. Scary, huh?

M. A little…

F. I would have liked to stay for longer.

M. I know. I'm just glad to see you now.

F. That's good. Me too.

M. We're gonna have a great… thirty-one hours… or whatever. I've everything sorted. You can just put yourself in my hands for the next while. Can you do that?

F. I think so.

M. I hate the airport.

F. This airport? JFK?

M. All airports are the same. I hate all airports.

F. How do we get out of here?

M. Shuttle bus to the subway.

F. Howard Beach JFK. The longest train I've ever seen.

M. And off through happy crappy Queens, before dipping down into darkness.

Lunch and Old Dynamic

M. My place is on Avenue A.

F. Ah, Alphabet City.

M. That's right. Guy in a bar told me a little ditty about Alphabet City.

F. Oh yeah?

M. Yeah. '*On Avenue A, you're alright. On B, you're brave. On C, you're crazy. And on D, you're dead.*'

F. Nice.

Pause.

You look good.

M. I do?

F. Yeah. Happy?

M. I guess, yeah. I fucking love this place.

F. You didn't feel that way in that email.

M. That was ages ago. I'd just arrived.

F. You said you were lonely. An anonymous speck in the mad bad city.

M. I suppose I felt that at first, but then...

F. But then?

M. You start to realise that being an anonymous speck in the mad bad city is pretty fucking liberating.

F. It is?

M. Trouble with Dublin, with Ireland, is, you can't move without bumping into someone you know.

F. The morning after a night on coke or something and here's your auntie coming out of SuperValu.

M. Exactly. No escape. Over here it's different.

F. Clean slate. Blank page.

M. More people between here and Harlem than in the whole of Ireland. The population of our entire country wedged into about a hundred and twenty city blocks. Think about it.

F. Crazy when you put it like that.

M. I love it.

Pause.

This is nice. I like this.

F. What?

M. This little banter. Easy and casual, like we just seen each other yesterday.

F. Why wouldn't it be? Hasn't been that long, has it?

M. Ah, a lot can happen in a few months.

F. Yeah. I guess.

   I thought about you the other day.

M. I feel privileged. What did you think about?

F. Some time we danced.

M. Oh yeah?

F. I wore a blue dress.

M. A blue dress?

F. Yes. Clingy. Sky blue.

M. Devil in a Blue Dress. When's this?

F. You don't remember? Before this. Then.

M. When?

F. A year or two ago. I danced with you.

M. Of course I remember dancing with you.

F. We were out.

M. Together.

F. Alone. Sort of... Not with the class. I didn't want to be at
   home then.

M. Great.

F. No. I enjoyed being with you too.

M. Hey, you're up to your knees, keep digging.

F. My mother wasn't happy then. Something was up. I'd come
   home and she'd be sitting in the kitchen. At the table.
   Sipping cups of cold tea.

M. What was wrong?

F. She wouldn't speak. I tried. I don't know. My brother?
   Sisters? My dad? She wouldn't speak. Just sat there. Dead
   smile on her face. And looking like she might cry but never
   actually doing it. I think, days like this. And then... I didn't
   want to be home any more.

M. So you came out with me.

F. No, I did want to be there. Something different. Some… what was it?

M. Dramasoc night, or…

F. That was the first night I really looked at you.

M. What?

F. I mean, I knew you before that. Your voice there. Talking to me. And a presence there. Whenever in college. But I never really looked at you until that night. Dancing with you.

M. And not jumping around techno shit. Hands clasped, spinning disco shit. Bee Gees. Cheesy but, fun. What the hell, we're eighteen.

F. Nineteen.

M. Yeah.

F. I looked at your face. Your eyes. A real intense blue. Hadn't noticed them before. Almost fake, so blue.

M. Fake eyes I have now?

F. On me, intense, even when you were having a laugh. Dancing.

M. Hey, you were smiling.

F. Yeah. I was. I was happy there. Dancing with you. Where was it again?

M. You don't remember where it was?

F. No.

M. You really wanna know?

F. Yeah.

M. Gonna ruin your nice image.

F. Really?

M. Yeah. You wanna know where that was? That was in Break for the fuckin Border.

F. No!

M. Yes!

F. Fuck, really? Break for the fuckin Border?

M. Yeah. A Tuesday night. Some dramasoc thing.

F. Fuck.

M. Ah, whatever, we were eighteen.

F. Nineteen.

Back to His Apartment

M. Let's drop your bag into my place. It's just around the corner.

F. Sure.

M. I gotta warn you, there's a lot of steps.

F. That's okay, you're carrying the bag.

M. You wanna take a shower?

F. That would be great.

M. You leave the door open. I watch you from the kitchen. Your body distorted by the clear plastic curtain.

F. Stiffness and stickiness from hours of travel wash away.

I enjoy your eyes on me.

M. You come out, wrapped in a towel, as I pop the cork of the Moët in celebration.

F. Just happened to have a bottle of champagne lying around?

M. For special occasions.

F. Like this?

M. Sure. I'm prepared. Bought champagne flutes in Macy's and everything.

F. And away you pour.

M. Both slouched coolly across the sofa. Sipping away.

F. Slipping away. Towel loose, hair wet.

M. Watching you rub creams into your skin.

F. Face and arms.

M. Neck and legs.

F. Your hand caresses the inside of my thigh.

M. 'Uh-uh,' you deny me, pushing my hand away.

F. I'm all clean. Maybe later.

Dinner

M. First stop. Dinner at Bar 89 in Soho.

F. You keep watching me sipping my drink.

M. What have you done to your eyes?

F. Mascara. Same as always.

M. Seem different. Darker. Bigger. You have big dark eyes.

F. Same as always. Always this dark. Always this big.

M. The colossal squid has the biggest eyes of any living creature on the planet. Black and dead and round. Able to see in total blackness. See everything. See things that cannot see you. That's you, that is. You're a colossal fucking squid...

F. Not quite sure what you mean by that. Is that an insult or an honest description?

M. You think I see you as a cold undulating sea creature?

F. I've been told I have an icy quality more than once.

Pause.

M. So has it been a busy summer for you?

F. How do you mean?

M. Any adventures? Romance?

F. I wouldn't say romance. Some fooling around.

M. Some fooling around?

F. You hardly expect me to go without sex for three months?

M. No. I guess not. Who'd you fool around with?

F. Well… There was a biker, who had a Harley. We rode to San Diego on it one weekend. I think he was more interested in that bike than me.

M. Anyone else?

F. A Scottish guy. And a surfer, of course. California, after all.

M. Of course.

F. The Scottish guy had something. He was older. Experienced. Very good with his tongue.

M. Really…

F. Yeah. Nothing too memorable though. Fleeting.

M. Not like our little fling?

F. No. Not like that. Not at all.

M. That's what we're calling it then?

F. A fling?

M. Yes.

F. I don't know what you'd call it.

M. I've thought about it – us – a lot.

F. Yeah, I bet you have.

M. Jesus, you're good, aren't you?

F. Too good?

M. You'll die alone.

F. Won't we all?

Carpo's

M. We take the N one stop up to 8th Street, then walk across to Bleecker and one of my favourite café's for dessert; Carpo's.

F. It's a cute little place that you can sit at tables outside and watch the Greenwich Village circus dancing merrily by.

M. I love this place, I swear the blueberry pie here gives me a boner, it's that good.

F. That's quite a recommendation.

M. Trust me, it's great.

Pause.

F. My mother's selling the pub.

M. Oh?

F. We thought we could hold on to it. But her heart's not in it and the guy she hired to manage the place was useless.

M. Why not get another guy?

F. No. She's made up her mind. Took her this long, but it's what she wants now. Move on somehow.

M. That's shitty. Sorry to hear that. I know that place meant so much to your family. To your dad.

F. But he's dead now.

M. Yeah.

F. Hard to believe it's been almost a year.

M. How has your mother been?

F. As good as. She's tough. Resilient. He was much older than her. She knew it would happen some day. That she'd be left behind.

M. Yeah but, still...

F. It meant so much to me, you being there at the funeral. You didn't have to be there.

M. A surprise.

F. Everyone else doing their solemn duty. Being bored and polite. Waiting for the pub. Unsure what to say. And you walk over.

M. Awkward and smiling. Hands in my pockets. Trying to catch your eye.

F. Wasn't really looking at people. Sick of their sober expressions and standard sympathies. All the double-handed handshakes. Then you walk over. So weird seeing you there.

M. Not sure what to do. Went to the mass. Saw you and your older sister speaking about him at the lectern.

F. The state of us.

M. No, it was beautiful what you said. You did really well.

F. No, the state of me. None of my gang hung around. A lot of them didn't even come.

M. Too cool for school.

F. Too awkward for something real.

M. Like death or...

F. You came to the pub with me. Stayed with me. The whole day. Not being serious. Laughing and talking. Meant a lot to me.

M. I'm glad.

F. You're stuck in some part of my head because of that.

M. I'm glad.

F. I'll always remember that. You walking over. Being there for me. When you hardly even knew me.

M. I knew you.

Pause.

You feel like dancing tonight?

F. Always feel like dancing.

M. We're on the guest list at Twilo. Sasha & Digweed.

F. Yeah? Class. Let's do it so.

To Twilo

M. In the subway you link my arm and give me a quick kiss on the lips that I'm not expecting.

F. This is a really good night.

M. Yeah.

F. I'm having such a good time.

M. Good. Me too.

F. I really needed this... everything I'm going back to... This is a great blowout to say goodbye.

M. Goodbye?

F. To America. Top it off, you know?

M. Streets getting noticeably darker this way.

F. Down West 27th Street.

M. Way, way west, practically in view of the highway.

F. Past the longest nightclub queue I've ever seen.

M. Groups and groups of yoked-up ravers…

F. Chancin-their-arm teenagers…

M. And besuited coke-heads and their blonde dates.

F. Chattering into their cellphones and handbags…

M.…and shivering against the shutters of garages and limo-rental joints.

F. All waiting for entry to Twilo.

M. Once again I marvel at the brilliance of being on the list.

F. Inside is dark and smoky, lit by lasers and black lights and glowsticks. And basically any crazy shit that glows in the dark.

M. A full-on bouncy electro rave.

F. Everyone well into it. Not giving a shit. Not pulling a pose.

M. Just dancing and dancing and sweating like fuck.

F. Class. Have to get some pills for this.

M. Really? I'm not so sure that's a good idea.

F. You're getting old.

M. Feel pretty far gone with all the alcohol, not sure I'm up for pills…

F. You don't want to do one? Not now? Not with me?

M. But you want to, so I'll do one, just to be on the same buzz, I guess. I watch you move across the dance floor.

F. Dancing through people. Free amongst the faces. Sweat and hair and arms flying. Everyone blissfully lost in the music.

M. You glide through them. So sexy. Neon-lit. Beautiful.

Pill Paranoia

F. And a little later, we're in a different part of the club.

M. Sofas, music lower, lights brighter, couples drinking and smoking, people talking. The chill-out room.

F. But you're anything but. Sitting there. Smoking. Looking around. Your eyes narrow.

M. Insect-like. Reptile-like. Unblinking.

F. Just watching. Watching me. Watching everything.

M. Vision's all stuttery. Jumping in and out of focus. That's why I'm sitting. Everything else is too complicated. And that's why I'm smoking. The burning tip of the cigarette, something to focus on, something that's in my control.

F. I'm talking to the guy who sold me the ecstasy. He's a young Asian guy with blond highlights. He's from Jersey and smiles a lot.

M. My eyes are slits. I am a reptile. I am a chameleon. Skin's tingling all over. Changing. Blending in with my surroundings, melting into the sofa. No one can see me. No one looking at me. No one talking to me. Not even you. I'm not here.

F. Breasts and spine starting to tingle with the mild come-up. I'm smiling too. The Asian guy talking about buses or something. Being a funny fuck. Still smiling. One tooth gold-plated.

M. I feel my long tongue flicking about inside my parched mouth. Coiled and ready to strike out at any of the brightly coloured insects around me. You're talking to one. A little down the sofa from me. Stuttery vision honed in on you. Every movement.

F. Not sure what he's telling me any more. But I'm laughing at whatever it is. Nodding to him. Looking down at my hands on my lap. My nails lightly tracing glowing orange trails over my bare thighs.

M. His eyes are watching your hands. Your thighs. You lean your face close to his ear. A whisper? What? He smiles, moves his head close to your ear, almost touching. I see his hand touch your thigh.

F. His hand is on my thigh. Cheeks twitch. Stuttery chemical rush behind my eyes.

M. Skin tingles painfully now. Some sort of madness burning up from inside. Camouflage disappears and I grow out of the couch.

F. All at once, a rush of displaced air and you're between us. Your face between us. Me and the smiling Asian guy from Jersey. Our faces lit faintly by the glow of your burning cigarette.

M. If you kiss her, I'll put this out on your eyeball.

F. Asian guy's smile fades. Eyes widen. Turns to me.

M. I stare at him. Don't blink or breathe.

F. 'Sorry, man, didn't realise that was your girlfriend,' Asian guy says and backs away.

M. I rise with him, cigarette still poised, watch him disappear into the crowd.

F. You sit back down beside me.

M. Did that just happen? Face is distorted in metal tabletop. Doesn't look like me. Looks crazy. Someone else. Not me.

F. What's wrong with you? I wasn't gonna kiss him. He's gay. I was just talking to him.

M. Don't say anything. Can't say anything.

F. Rushes turning to shivers. I can't look at you. Can't move.

M. I want you to be angry at me. To laugh at me. Anything other than you looking so scared. Scared of me.

F. I need air.

M. You want to get out of here?

Yaffa Café

F. The taxi drops us at a place near your apartment called the Yaffa Café. We get a tiny table by a painted statue of Buddha, under the watchful eyes of dead Jim Morrison.

M. Have you talked to anyone from college since you left?

F. No.

M. No one?

F. What's the point? Done with that. Finished. College friends are college friends. Don't mean that much, once you're through.

M. You won't stay friends with any of them?

F. Don't think so. Will you?

M. Yeah, I think so. Some of them.

F. I don't think you will.

M. Why?

F. Can't stay in contact with everyone you meet. Even good friends drift apart. Over time. Only natural. You do new things. Go new places. Meet new people.

M. That's depressing.

F. No, it's not.

M. It is. Three years in college with people you're never going to see again.

F. You'll pass them on the street. Dublin's small after all. The world's small too. Meet them on a beach in Thailand or Australia or something. Everyone ends up there eventually.

M. Thailand?

F. Australia. India. Wherever.

M. When did you get so cynical?

F. I think I was about… seven.

M. You don't think any of the college people are worth keeping in contact with?

F. No. What do we have in common now, except the past?

More Drugs?

F. You want to know why I was talking to that guy?

M. The guy in Twilo?

F. Yeah.

M. Why?

F. I wanted to get some coke. I felt like some coke.

M. And?

F. And he had some. He gave it to me. He was off his head. He gave it to me for nothing. Cos I'm Irish. Cos I'm fabulous. Something… You wanna a do a line or two? Keep the come-down at bay?

M. We take turns in the tiny bathroom of the Yaffa, cutting out lines on the dirty toilet-roll dispenser.

F. Ever so glamorous this.

M. But fuck, a blast up either nostril gives me the jolt of life that I need right now.

F. Knocking the exhausted come-down feeling out of me and carrying me back to our little table feeling all sparkly again.

M. The room seems to shimmer around us.

F. Everything covered in glitter.

M. And the wine goes down in nice thick gulps.

F. And it's all smiles and rosy cheeks and excited chatter for a while.

M. Until you start to look a little yellow.

F. And your smile has been replaced by clenched teeth and your eyes are bloodshot and raw.

M. As the uncertainty creeps back.

I really freaked myself out by what I said to that guy in the club. That was just mental. I'm not like that. I'm not jealous. I just… I haven't seen you in so long and a lot of feelings came back to me and the E was messing with my head and… I'm really, really sorry. I'll never do or say anything like that again.

F. Look, I said it was okay. Okay? You don't have to apologise again. It was freaky, you did scare me. But we're off our faces. Mad shit happens. Let's just forget about it, okay?

M. Okay. It's forgotten.

F. Good.

M. And it is. We drink some coffee and share a slice of pie.

F. And do the rest of the coke.

M. The guilt I feel beginning to lessen.

F. I think the only other thing we can do tonight is go home and pass out.

M. We pay the bill and leave.

Blood in the Hallway

F. Laughing, barely able to walk.

M. Crawling up the steps of my apartment building.

F. Starting to crash. Stumbling through into the narrow fluorescent hallway.

M. I catch you before you slide down the wall.

F. Laughing. Lost. Fucked. Pulling you towards me.

M. Kissing me.

F. Yeah and sort of passing out at the same time. Stars and shit behind my eyelids. I open them. You're looking at me funny. Disgust or worry?

M. There's blood. A dark crimson trail from your nostril to your lips.

F. Shit.

M. Are you okay?

F. Do you have a tissue?

M. What happened?

F. It's okay. It's nothing.

M. Nothing? I give you a crumpled tissue from my jacket pocket.

F. Wipe away the blood. Laugh again. Stars again. Head back. Fucking beautiful.

M. Too much coke?

F. Too much of everything. You hold me and I lean into you. Propped against the wall. I close my eyes and wait for the sound of the door opening.

M. But I don't open it because I'm looking at you.

F. What's left of me. A mess. I'm dissolving into this decrepit wallpaper. I can't open my eyes. My stomach is burning. I rub it.

M. You look out of focus. A smudged photograph. Your scruffy hands smooth the shimmering grey fabric of your dress. And slowly you slide the hem of your dress up your bare thighs. I sink slowly to the cold tiles of the landing.

F. There's some trace of the ecstasy or maybe just the coke and alcohol circulating inside of me. A fuzzy liquid electricity that makes my skin shiver. Beautifully. To your touch. Your fingers on my calves.

M. And travelling slowly higher. Magnetised. The smell of you. Wine. Smoke. Sweat. Perfume. The heat from between your legs glowing close to my face. I close my eyes and sink into that warmth. Tasting you.

F. Disappearing completely. Melting into a puddle of chemicals. Natural and otherwise. Working their magic.

M. Dissolving into a warm, black welcoming void.

Post Coital

F. My mother told me: don't trust men.

M. They only want your body.

F. And they only want it for a short time too.

M. Then they want someone else.

F. Don't trust them. Ever.

M. She's a wise woman.

F. Yes.

M. Think your dad only wanted her for her body?

F. She was good to him. She gave him everything. She gave him four daughters and one son.

M. Who's a little gone in the head.

F. You would be too if you had four sisters.

M. I think I love you.

F. You think?

M. I love you.

F. Don't say that.

M. It's what I feel.

F. You're still drunk. We've had sex. We're sleeping together. I'm warm. Feel good beside you. That's what you feel. That's all you feel.

M. I know what I feel. You're scared of that.

F. I'm not scared of anything.

M. What's wrong then?

F. I just don't want to hear that from you now.

M. Then when?

F. You hardly even know me.

M. What are you talking about? Of course I know you.

F. No, you don't.

M. I know you. Jesus, come on.

F. Why do you think you love me?

M. I don't think, I—

F. What is it about me you love?

M. You're different. You're special. Everyone else is so ordinary.

F. I'm not special. There's nothing special about me. I'm a mess. I'm a waste.

M. What? You don't know yourself. I think you're perfect. I think you're incredible. I can't stop looking at you. When you're not here, I keep seeing you. I hear your voice in my head. Things you've said. Your voice. Stored in there.

F. You're mad.

M. I know.

F. No, you're really crazy.

M. You're crazy. I can't believe you don't realise the effect you have on me.

F. I'm tired.

M. So am I.

F. Go to sleep, please.

M. Silence. Black, cold, silence.

In Dreams

F. Colours and shapes begin to form behind my dark eyelids.

M. The street sounds outside change. Fade.

F. Merge. Swelling sounds. Waves. The sound of water. The ocean. Sounds in the centre of my head at first. And then all around me. By the ocean.

M. I'm holding your hand. Where are we? Moving downstairs. The stairwell. You're smiling at me. Happy. Fresh. Out on the dark street now. Moving through pools of light from the lamps. Night-time in New York.

F. Lying on a beach of soft white sand. Sun low in the sky in front of me. Setting. Tilting palms lilting behind me. A warm breeze through paradise. Thailand or somewhere I haven't been to yet. Yet here I am now. On the beach. By myself.

M. We're going down steps again. A subway station. Through the turnstiles and still holding your hand. Never letting go. Warm and clammy and familiar.

F. I say by myself but what I mean is, I am alone. There are many other people on the beach. But they are not with me. And the sun is definitely setting now, so people are starting to leave. But it's still almost perfect. Warm and shimmering and…

M. Inside on the platform. Eerily quiet. Echoes from the tunnel. We sit down on a bench together. Warm breeze from the tunnel mouth. Then footsteps. Voices. Three big guys. Blocking our exit. Scowling, grinning trouble. Shit.

F. My skin is different. Tanned, taut. Aged. Burned. Toughened. I'm older. A woman. A middle-aged woman. Lying here in the sun on this beach. In Thailand or wherever, I haven't been there yet…

M. They're up in our face now. You and me. We're standing now. Surrounded by these guys. Trying to talk with them. Reason with them. They want our money. They want what we have. We give it to them. But they want more. They shove me back onto the bench. A punch. A kick. One of them grabs your arm.

F. I watch a little blonde girl playing near the edge of the clear blue water. She splashes her hands in the sea, happily, laughing to herself. I feel my tired face spread into a smile and watch as she comes out of the sea and runs across the sand.

M. The two bigger guys are holding me down. Can't breathe. The smaller one, the leader, is pulling at your dress, off your shoulder, until— A fast vicious movement. You shove him, with all your strength, in the chest. He stumbles back off the edge of the platform.

F. The little girl runs past me. Her mammy and daddy sitting up near the tree line. The man seems… It's you. The little girl is your daughter. You sitting there on the sand. You look the same. As I remember you. You haven't aged. Boyish still.

M. He hits the tracks hard. His head clattering against the electric track. Sending volts and volts of electric blasts through his body. The other two release me to turn and watch their friend's body begin to smoke below the platform. His eyeballs explode with a wet pop.

F. You and your little women. Cute little daughter. Perfect little wife. Younger than me. She looks like she loves you more than breathing. A happy little unit. You don't recognise me. Don't even see me here. Staring until it hurts. Your happiness blinding me.

M. Your hand is suddenly in mine again, dragging me quickly from the bench and down the platform in a blur of frantic motion. You're so wild and strong and exciting. I'd do anything for you. Go anywhere with you. Escape all this. Together. To freedom. To paradise. Thailand, or somewhere… bright. So bright… as…

Waking Up

F. Morning comes.

M. Breaking and entering through the bedroom window.

F. Muscling aside the venetian blinds and glaring up the room with white fire.

M. A dozen taxicabs honking away outside in a no-honking zone.

F. And construction workers drilling at a crack in the side of my skull.

M. Breakfast conversation is light and transparent.

F. Tired but friendly.

M. Making fun of the songs on the radio.

F. Not really looking at each other much.

M. And eating even less.

F. I dress in my travelling clothes while you're in the shower.

M. And we leave the apartment dazed and silent.

Central Park

F. It rains in the afternoon.

M. A heavy wet autumnal downpour.

F. You open up the umbrella and hold me close under it as we cross into the park.

M. Japanese tourists in plastic rain ponchos are taking photos of the John Lennon memorial.

F. Flowers of red and purple and yellow lay around the circular plaque, taking a heavy battering from the aggressive sheets of rain.

M. We move down a curving path and follow the Park Drive for a while. As we emerge from an awning of trees you shrug my arm off your shoulder and move a little ahead of me.

F. It's okay, it's not really raining any more.

Museum

M. On the east side of Central Park is the Metropolitan Museum of Art.

F. Inside the museum is very busy. Lots of children and tourists.

M. We wander around the massive buidling in a daze.

F. Pausing every once in a while to examine pieces that we recognise.

M. Downstairs is a reconstructed Egyption temple.

F. Dedicated to Isis and Osiris, the Temple of Dendur.

M. I smile and reach out to take your hand as we look down into the reflecting pool around the temple.

F. Without looking at you, I slip my hand free and move on.

M. We move on through a hall of various armour from around the world. I can't stop thinking about why you won't hold my hand.

F. Behind me you stop and sit down opposite a large samurai.

Why did you stop?

M. I don't know.

F. Are you okay?

M. I'm fine. Just a little tired.

F. I thought...

M. What?

F. I was after upsetting you or something. I thought you were... crying?

M. No, just... tired.

F. You smile and get up from the bench, walking alongside me again.

It's closing time soon.

M. Yeah.

F. We should go.

M. Yeah.

F. Let's go.

M. Okay.

To Newark

M. The evening traffic on 42nd Street is light and it only takes a few minutes to cross under the Hudson via the Lincoln Tunnel.

F. We emerge into the bright sunset in a different state.

M. New Jersey. Up ahead huge jumbo jets criss-cross low over the expressway.

F. And we soon pull into Newark Departures.

M. Back in the airport again. I hate the airport.

F. You said that before.

M. I know. I still hate it.

F. We get some McDonald's and a seat by the window.

M. Watching the blinking lights and the onset of darkness beyond.

Pause.

I had to say that to you last night. That is how I feel.

F. I know.

M. And you don't…

F. I don't know what I feel any more. If I feel anything at all.

M. Of course you do.

F. I feel broken. I feel empty. Since last year. Before that even.

M. I don't believe that.

F. You should. By now.

M. Yeah… Nearly the end of September. Weird not to be going back to college.

F. College is over. The real world for us now.

M. It's always been real.

F. I'm sorry…

M. Don't be.

F. I just can't…

Pause.

It was a great weekend.

M. Memorable?

F. Yes.

M. Still there…

F. Still holding tight.

M. A moment. Too long.

F. Until boarding is announced.

M. This is not the last time I'll see you.

F. But it is the last time I'll speak to you.

M. The last time I'll hold you.

F. Is this all it was?

M. A brief stopover?

F. On the way from somewhere.

M. To someplace else.

F. Another time and place entirely.

M. Is this all it was?

F. Well, it's still here…

M. We're still there… How real was this?

F. I say goodbye.

M. I say… I say… *I stay.*

The End.

WHEN COWS GO BOOM

Stacey Gregg

STACEY GREGG

Stacey Gregg's other plays include *I'm Spilling My Heart Out Here*, produced as part of the National Theatre's Connections Festival in 2013, *Override* for the Watford Palace Theatre in 2013, and *Lagan* at Ovalhouse, London, in 2011. Her previous work at the Abbey Theatre includes *Perve*, which premiered on the Peacock stage in 2011, and *Shibboleth*, a co-commission with the Goethe Institut and the Abbey Theatre, which had a reading directed by Conall Morrison on the Peacock stage as part of the 2010 Ulster Bank Dublin Theatre Festival. *When Cows Go Boom* was presented on the Peacock stage as part of the 20:Love series of public readings in 2008. Her first play *Ismene* was shortlisted for the Royal Court Young Writers Festival. She was subsequently on attachment at RADA, and commissioned through Rough Magic's SEEDS programme to develop *Grand Tour*. Stacey also writes for screen and is developing an original television series and a one-off drama.

When Cows Go Boom was first performed as a rehearsed reading as part of the 20:Love play-reading series for the Abbey Theatre, Dublin, in 2008. The cast was as follows:

MAN	Emmet Kirwan
WOMAN	Fiona Bell
Director	Rachel West

Characters

MAN
WOMAN

References: the Niger Delta oil conflict, and the Shell to Sea campaign, County Mayo, Ireland.

shadow people

A row of various plastic containers.

Two figures, faces obscured, push wheelbarrows in the half-dark.

Now they are moving toward one another.

They recognise each other, gesture. One reaches out.

Explosion.

bomb giver

A home, a village.

A WOMAN *sits, humming, scratching something onto a stone.*

A MAN *in uniform stands slightly apart.*

Around are strewn plastic containers. A wheelbarrow.

A cock crows somewhere outside.

She stops humming.

He fiddles with his pass.

WOMAN   See my garden? On the way in? Nothing I used to like more than tootling up and down, tending the herbs. My husband would take off his shirt in the sun. The kids would help. There'd be stew...

        She smiles. The MAN *is silent, stony.*

        Not much to look at, now. Overran, the weeds. That's what a weed does, devastates other life...

She looks for a response from him.

I'm a great one for metaphors, notice?

He spits and cleans the tip of his shoe.

Told you I was an idiot, no doubt.

She squints at him.

Do I know you?

He looks off.

It's the nose. A significantnose. I'd know that nose anywhere.

A beat.

MAN   (*Dismissive.*) No.

WOMAN   You'd know my father –

MAN   don't know you.

WOMAN   Your father was the fisherman

MAN   he had a boat

WOMAN   – cos he was the fisherman, course he had a boat

MAN   just had a boat

WOMAN   That changes things, doesn't it. Well I didn't expect that. It's the nose.

           She measures him with an attentive eye.

           You married one of those girls – gorgeous bunch. Full-lipped, strong-boned, but slight when they turned sidewards —

MAN   No.

WOMAN   wasn't she very beautiful, now? Oval eyes, like nuts. Big – (*Gestures, breasts.*)

MAN   Look –

WOMAN   Lovely.

Lull. A hazy smile on her face.

She scratches at the stone.

The MAN *shuffles.*

MAN   (*Despite himself.*) You knew my wife?

WOMAN   O yes, Nut Eyes, you took her to the dance at the community hall.

He nods.

Summer before it burnt down, beautiful bright-blue day – someone'd brewed something, Old Fella couped sideways in his seat, singing, someone threw a pot of piss round him to shut him up haha – you and her round the back of the hall. I was too embarrassed to interrupt –

The MAN *leans in.*

When someone dies
Feels. Strange things. Continue.

The MAN *is still again.*

Can't stop talking – (*Touches her mouth.*) a, a tiredness. I've my ma's mouth. Her mother's mouth. Last thing I saw of her, her mouth. Was looking at her closed dead mouth, how it looked like mine, all tight and closed.

You've your father's eyes. Bright, hard. Blue. Shock to see someone's eyes in a different face. (*Firm.*) You had pyjamas with giraffes on them.

MAN   (*Quickly.*) Bullshit.

WOMAN   Tt. What did we teach you…

Beat.

Your father played the spoons, we'd fall round laughing, BigNose / plays the spoons

MAN   What?

WOMAN   Yes!

MAN   You're inventing –

WOMAN   Inventing?

MAN   No one played the spoons.

WOMAN   Dear, you wouldn't remember, you weren't here. You left, after they put the pipes down — a straw in someone else's drink, I always said. Bled us dry.

MAN   My dad wasn't musical

WOMAN   You were a greedy nipper with a straw. (*Sudden*.) I watched them leave, last night – shuttup now I'm telling you something – made them sandwiches, the nippers. Wrapped them, one by one. I, my hands were shaking. (*To herself*.) The little ones should've taken coats.

The MAN *is disgusted.*

Your uncle was among them. Did you love him?

MAN   Never knew him.

WOMAN   They went to my sister's village.
Way the pipe runs.
I understand you, cos you loved that girl, why I let you in my home…

She leans over, brushes his hair with her hand.

Remember you courting. My sister left around that time. Hard, her leaving. Like a limb gone. Like breaking up with your first sweetheart. It dulls, but. Goes away. Begin to worry about what's for dinner again. Out of sight out of mind – feel less, ahm, responsible. Do you love your wife?

MAN   she lies in my back. Can't sleep unless…

He stops, surprised by his own words.

WOMAN   Yes. Must be difficult working in the plant. You go
          home some weekends?

MAN   Sometimes.

          Pause.

          Not enough.

WOMAN   Your family though, you do it to support / them

MAN   Don't patronise me.

WOMAN   I'm not.

          Pause.

          How's work then? Tell me about your job. Read
          much?

          MAN *shakes his head,*

          No. Me neither. Keep the books in the fridge. Not
          much good for anything else, they never
          connected us. Useless. Doesn't even keep them
          cold, the books, / hah.

MAN   Nothing to do with me.

WOMAN   Sun's going in, they'll be here soon.

          He looks at his watch.

          Looks at the door, expectant.

          Always were a bit. What age were you when they
          told us to sell up?

MAN   (*Automatic.*) Twelve.

WOMAN   Same age as my daughter. Need a good thump at
          that age.

          She goes back to scratching the stone.

          Tell me about the plant.

          Silence.

(*Suddenly brisk, chatty.*) Remember the old judge? You should, the pig locked our daddies away – well his wife was good friends with the oil men. I'll be honest, if someone shit in my nice front room (if I had a nice front room) I'd be upset. But if someone shit in my neighbour's I'd take an interest, but not *too* bothered, not overly worried. If they shit in another county, well, that's just not worth wasting your time over it's probably not even real shit – life's too short isn't it? Life's too short. (*Harder.*) I want to hear about the plant. You can see it from here. I could probably see you if you waved from your window. Well I'm exaggerating. Not one contract for us, and the size of it. No grouting to be done? No windows to be washed, concrete mixed, nothing? No chrome to be buffed? No one wanted to rock the boat, few skulls cracked on the picket line teaches a quick lesson. Had a toe broke, in all the scuffling, didn't you? Poor thing. Back when we bothered scuffling. Is that when you took the job?

MAN   baby was starving

WOMAN   Oh I know, they bought up everything

MAN   work dried up

WOMAN   I know, the infants had only stones to play with, the farm was gone. Must've been hard. Was it hard? You broke your mother's heart as well / as your toe

MAN   I had a wife, a baby.

WOMAN   yes.

MAN   a woman and a – stop nodding

WOMAN   why?

MAN   stop nodding – *idiots* – blew yourselves up, / *idiots*

WOMAN   Just

MAN   Listen

WOMAN   I *heard* you

MAN   I COULDN'T'VE come back, they'd've beaten
          me, abducted me – / they'd've taken me hostage

WOMAN   oh don't be so self-important, you always were a
          pompous child.

          Pause.

          Your kids are alive, so there you go.

          The WOMAN *looks away. Miles away.*

MAN   Can I have water?

          He wants to demand it, but can't.

          A beat.

          *She pours from a plastic container into a colourful
          tumbler.*

          He takes it, takes a gulp.

          He chokes, spits it out, stands retching.

WOMAN   (*Lightly.*) Feed that to my babies. You shit in that.
          Your father would know, the fish are all dead.
          Belly up.

          The MAN *tosses the tumbler at her.*

          Tell me about the shower!

MAN   Eugh – BITCH

WOMAN   Describe it! In the plant, go on! I'm asking nice.

          He spits.

MAN   It's in a block –

WOMAN   A block? There's several?

MAN   YES.

WOMAN   Several showers.

MAN   Sinks. (*Vindictive*.) Loads.

WOMAN   is it hot?

MAN   sometimes –

WOMAN   what

MAN   it's *too* hot.

WOMAN   sometimes it's too hot? Do you drink it?

MAN   no

WOMAN   why? Cos it's too hot?

MAN   cos there're taps

WOMAN   ah. And they'll be almost *too* cold

MAN   if you let the water run it gets colder, like ice.

WOMAN   what happens to the water?

MAN   …

WOMAN   the water you're not drinking…

            He turns from her. The WOMAN *giggles.*

            How *lovely.* What else. Tell me something else.
            Tell me about going to the toilet there

MAN   …?

WOMAN   do you piss in the toilet? Shit?

MAN   yes I / shit

WOMAN   you shit in the toilet. And then, you don't shit on it
            again, you flush it away. Magic. Invisible. No shit.
            No shit at all. Your shit probably doesn't even
            leave a smell.

            The MAN *throws one of the plastic containers at
            her.*

MAN   (*Shouts.*) You put those in their arms.
            KIDS. SENT THEM OUT, WALKING BOMBS.

WOMAN   We could've cleaned them toilets.
             My husband was a biochemist. Educated man but
             they built the road to the city, *left us off*, took
             what's ours and left us *off the road* – but I see I
             see I see you can't connect 'terrorists' to the grid
             we get a fridge to put books in all is forgiven –
             we're animals – I'm a terrible terrorist. I'm a
             terrible terror. Terribly / terrible la la la

MAN   Shut up shut up.

WOMAN   Last night, by the light of gas flares – I was in the
             rain, watching the plant, glow – (*Remembering,
             soft.*) like some kind of – heavenly, some kind of
             heaven. Miles, only thing you can see. Glows.
             What I thought Heaven looks like.

             He is pacing, agitated.

MAN   They gave you programmes, to develop the – you
             all signed up

WOMAN   (*Laughs.*) words / words –

MAN   changed your minds –

WOMAN   That's what you do when you're picking flowers –
             they said we were kidnapping.

MAN   but then you did!

WOMAN   any excuse for a forceful hand.

MAN   You *tortured* – the police told / us you tortured
             them

WOMAN   'Police'? The private security? The heavies?

MAN   I just do data entry.

WOMAN   You're the spark.

MAN   I have a family –

WOMAN   You're the spark that kills.

MAN   You murdered *kids*.

WOMAN   Tell me then. Your family –

MAN   – my wife, four children –

WOMAN   tell me. (*Desperate.*) Please. Tell me about love. You're a guest in my home. I knew you in giraffe pyjamas. Knew your young wife. While we were losing faith in democracy, you ran away. Pretend not to know me. You sit there. Explain. Please. I loved them…

          These people, these powerful bosses somewhere – don't they have a family?

MAN   fucking baby talk.

WOMAN   (*Sad.*) That's what my husband would've said.

MAN   Think I'm much better off?

WOMAN   Poor thing.

          I'm putting her name on this stone. Put where her remains are. If there are any. Held her head. (*Demonstrating.*) Looked in the eyes of my sister and. I'm here. (*Absent.*) I'm still here.

          A knock at the door.

          He turns, relieved.

          Her head wasn't. Only bit I could. In there.

          The wheelbarrow. He grimaces, backs away.

          They're here for me?

          She reaches out to him.

          I know you're finding this hard.

          The MAN *ducks from her touch.*

MAN   I – I'll tell them I know you.

WOMAN   You told me you don't know me.

MAN   (*Husky.*) They do favours, for family.

          A knock. He tries to leave.

WOMAN   Sorry – wait.

He stops.

You remember me. (*She nods: you do.*)
She said you were kind.

The MAN *is staring at the barrow, rooted, hands clasp and unclasp.*

Your wife. She was helping. Last night. Sorry.

Fade.

The WOMAN *standing under a tattered umbrella, watching, devastated, still.*

218. 218. Cars, loaded with dead.
We stole their shiny, shiny cars. Carry the corpses.
The kids should've taken coats.
Glows like Heaven. The plant.

Sound of rain.

proximity

Elsewhere. A MAN *and a* WOMAN *in suits, smoothie each, with a straw. Sheltering under an umbrella.*

WOMAN   Cos once you make a decision

MAN   I know

WOMAN   You're stuck with it.

MAN   I know, I know

WOMAN   I know you know

MAN   Pressure.

WOMAN   Perspective.

MAN   Doesn't it –

WOMAN	I mean –
MAN	make you re-evaluate?
WOMAN	current circumstances, investments, the future. When do you have to – ?
MAN	Make the decision by? Next week.
WOMAN	Wow. Tell me the –
MAN	The spec? 5.3 litre, 130 HP
WOMAN	roof rails?
MAN	Mm-hm
WOMAN	tinted glass, metallic red, temperature-activated AC
MAN	dash is sweet
WOMAN	fancy little cup-holders
MAN	fuck that, 'a tough-truck look hiding behind it is the heart of a passenger vehicle'
WOMAN	'The Survivor.' Sexy. Shiny. Shit.
MAN	Same as Josh's, chrome bumpers to buff, voice-activated navigation for when Megan goes to the shops and gets lost.
WOMAN	How is little Megan?
MAN	Not so little.
WOMAN	No they don't stay little
MAN	Blink and you miss it
WOMAN	Know what she wants to, you know, do?
MAN	International development, she was talking about.
WOMAN	Good for her. Something international relations-y –
MAN	the new media studies.
WOMAN	Well I know a diplomat friend if she ever – you know: Michael.

MAN   Tall Michael?

WOMAN   Tall Mike. Bendy Mike. And Tom?

MAN   Tom! Practically a hippy. Started some thing at
           school, the 'Ally Group' – for 'friends of gays',
           pffff I don't know.

WOMAN   Ha.

MAN   Don't know where he gets it from… pfff.

           Pause.

WOMAN   All this crap in schools, what do we teach them.

MAN   Hey ho.

WOMAN   All this crap and you handshaking and censuring –

MAN   Don't – you know / I have to

WOMAN   Handshaking and / censuring

MAN   Godsake

WOMAN   I'm not – I mean, it's just those things you say

MAN   It's not me, it's policy, we give them libraries –
           you're an intelligent woman, don't – I just head
           the campaign

WOMAN   The curriculum – what's 'unnatural' –

MAN   Keep your bloody voice down.

WOMAN   'immoral' –

MAN   I know you're finding this hard, but…

           Silence.

           She laughs involuntarily to herself.

           Meeting with Comms tomorrow.

WOMAN   Oh the thing.

MAN   Yesterday. Bunkering –

WOMAN	But it was their own, wasn't it? They'll only pick up on it if there were any of our guys. Were there any of our guys?
MAN	God, no, few plant workers, villagers with sticks
WOMAN	Some have guns.
MAN	Media haven't picked it up. Still raining? Mightn't go.
WOMAN	To the meeting?
MAN	Yeah look, raining.
WOMAN	Nightmare. Definite mizzle. Get a taxi.

He looks at the rain.

MAN	Kind of pretty. Light pollution. Glowy.
WOMAN	Don't go.

Their eyes meet.

MAN	Might be posted out there. Shower better be hot this time.
WOMAN	They're sending you out?
MAN	I've to wait –
WOMAN	To hear?
MAN	Yes.
WOMAN	Oh.
MAN	Yes.
WOMAN	How long?
MAN	No idea. Long as it takes. Some big thing – photos, girl wandering round in her underwear –
WOMAN	From the explosion?
MAN	No – I already said – the press *haven't* picked up on it – cos of these pictures – some reality-society

girl off her tits at some awards, front page.
Anyway. (*Beat*.) Hard on Jules.

WOMAN   Yeah.

MAN   Out of sight out of mind.

WOMAN   Yikes.

MAN   Was thinking of popping the question.

          Silence.

WOMAN   You're a good guy.

          Beat. He tries to read her, but can't.

MAN   Heard how it happened?

WOMAN   ?

MAN   The explosion.

WOMAN   Oh.

MAN   They reckon two wheelbarrows full of, you know,
          the siphoned stuff, the stolen oil – and because it
          was so dark – may've bumped into each other –
          sparked – Boom – wipe out – cows everywhere.

WOMAN   Wheelbarrows. *Plastic pots*. Insane.

MAN   Two hundred and eighteen dead. Just like that.
          Boom. Crackdown on resistance.

WOMAN   They always say that. I'm gonna get a stew to take
          away.

MAN   Here?

WOMAN   Yeah. Fancy?

MAN   No. Poison. Look, I've to go.

WOMAN   Do you?

MAN   Nice to bump into you. Pleasure as always.

WOMAN   Don't go.

MAN   See you later.

WOMAN   Bar?

MAN   Not tonight.

           He takes a playful sip from her straw.

           He pecks her on the cheek.

           Love to hubbyandkids.

WOMAN   Same. (*Tiny.*) I love you.

MAN   Cheer up.

           He goes. She watches.

           Her phone buzzes.

           Answering the phone with one hand as she goes.

WOMAN   (*Lying.*) Yeah I'm uh, stuck in traffic,
           sweetheart... well, make her take her coat... well,
           she should've worn a coat...

crucible

A body, mid-explosion, suspended.

BODY   I'm preparing stew.
           Something, bumps:
           explodes my pink body
           Clothes. Disintegrate.
           All distinguishing features,
           all hungry days longing for death and now
           in one breath
           split.
           Spilt.
           No time to cry
           so, I smile.

At the point of erasure.
The radius is very wide.
Arm rips from socket,
nerves, bone,
eyes – wide, shrivel into sockets,
wounds flower,
heart beat twice before arrest
and my soul
blazed out my scream to you, sister –
your beloved's
guts rain on your feet.
Each child, given a pot to fill,
each clutch its feeble bomb.
Black, black, slop.

They're unable to find my leg. Bury me without it.

Two kids, see each other, are reminded of kind
words and the bind of kin and pass a smile in eyes
and think of child-days;
But the path is rough, the men levelled it in the
dead of night, in the dark, things are uneven
in the dark, shapes mean nothing;
Path, littered with stones,
they reach,
barrows
Bump,
spark;
spark ignites oil
everyone dead.
My head detaches from my neck.
Blinks twice.

VOICES	bump
BODY	boom
VOICE	erased
	bump
	Beat.

Bump

Beat.

Bump

Beat.

(bump)

The body is gone.

Dripping. Leaves rustle.

Plastic containers, scattered.

LOVE IN A GLASS JAR

Nancy Harris

NANCY HARRIS

Nancy Harris was recipient of The Rooney Prize for Irish Literature and the Stewart Parker Trust New Playwright Bursary in 2012. Her work at the Abbey Theatre includes *No Romance*, which premiered on the Peacock stage in 2011. Other theatre credits include *Our New Girl* (Bush Theatre, London); *The Man With the Disturbingly Smelly Foot* (Unicorn Theatre, London); *Journey to X* (National Theatre Connections); *The Kreutzer Sonata* (Gate Theatre, London) and *Little Dolls* (Bush Theatre Broken Space Season). *Love in a Glass Jar*, her short-play commission for the 20:Love series of public readings, was presented on the Peacock stage in 2008. She has also been a writer on attachment at the Soho Theatre and National Theatre Studio, London, respectively, and was the Pearson Playwright in Residence at the Bush Theatre, London, in 2011. She has also written for radio and television.

Love in a Glass Jar was first performed as a rehearsed reading as part of the 20:Love play-reading series for the Abbey Theatre, Dublin, in 2008. The cast was as follows:

EVE   Karen Ardiff
PATRICK   Bosco Hogan

Director   Wayne Jordan

Characters

EVE, *late thirties*
PATRICK, *late forties*

Dialogue

…indicates an unfinished or unarticulated thought.

/ indicates an overlap in dialogue.

– indicates a pause or a beat where a thought is being clarified.

A hotel room in a boutique hotel, an hour outside of Dublin.

The room is minimalist to the point of stark – there is a double bed, a bedside table, a mini-bar, a window and a half-open door leading into a bathroom.

There is also a framed Andy Warhol print on the wall.

PATRICK *is standing looking at it, holding a near-empty glass in his hand.*

EVE *enters the room quietly from the outside hall. She catches sight of* PATRICK *staring at the print. She hesitates for a brief moment, then smiles and lets out a mock gasp.*

EVE. Oh my God you've still got your clothes on.

PATRICK. Pardon?

EVE. I don't know where to look.

PATRICK. What?

EVE. I'm just – joking. Sorry. It was a – it was a joke.

PATRICK. Oh. Right.

EVE. I've always wanted to say that to a man in a hotel room.

PATRICK. Which?

EVE. 'Oh my God you've still got your clothes on.' Or something like that. You know because… of what people get up to in hotels. Supposedly.

PATRICK. Right. Yes.

She moves away from the door, a little embarrassed.

EVE. It sounded much better in my head.

PATRICK. No. I got it. It was /

EVE. Stupid. I'm not Mae West. Never mind. You got yourself a drink?

PATRICK. I did, yeah, there's a mini-bar.

EVE. There's everything. It's boutique, apparently. The rooms don't even have numbers.

PATRICK. Oh? What do they have?

EVE. Moods. We're Serenity.

PATRICK. Good. (*Gesturing to the mini-bar.*) Would you like something from the...

EVE. No, thanks. Bit early for me. The girl at reception said we have until noon, but I told them you'd a train tonight so – you know. Thought I should say something in case they think I'm a bit of an old – slut or whatever.

She laughs nervously.

PATRICK. I don't think we should concern ourselves too much with what they think.

EVE. No. No, you're right, we shouldn't. It's just... she gave me a brochure.

I don't know why I took it. There are some lovely walks around this area she said. I know we won't, but I said we might because – well, I don't know why I said it actually.

PATRICK. Because otherwise she might have thought you a bit wanton.

EVE. Probably.

PATRICK. And you know the old saying – a wanton woman never wants a walk.

EVE. Is that an old saying?

PATRICK. No.

EVE. Oh.

Beat.

Well. I don't know how you like to do these things –
ordinarily.

PATRICK. I don't do these things ordinarily.

EVE. No. Me neither. Obviously.

PATRICK. You'll have to excuse me. I'm a bit nervous. It's
why I had the drink. It isn't a problem so you don't need to
concern yourself.

EVE. I wasn't.

PATRICK. Alcoholism doesn't run in my family or anything.
My parents barely drank at all.

EVE. Okay.

PATRICK. Just in case you were wondering. Just in case you
were thinking 'oh God, here's a man who can't be left in a
hotel room for five seconds without him guzzling the
contents of the mini-bar' –

EVE. No /

PATRICK. Cos I wouldn't. I might have another though, in a
minute – if that's alright? It won't affect my ability to – you
know. So don't worry.

EVE. That's – fine.

PATRICK. And I'll give you some money too. Wouldn't want
you to think I was a mean drunk.

He tries for a laugh.

EVE. Don't worry about money. I've left them my credit card,
it's all taken care of.

EVE *goes to the bed, where she picks up a small weekend
bag and starts looking inside.*

Have you had a look round?

PATRICK. I've had a bit of one.

EVE. How's the bathroom? I love hotel bathrooms.

PATRICK The bathroom is – well, it's a bit confused really.

EVE. How do you mean 'confused'?

PATRICK. Decor-wise. I mean there's a Botticelli in there
hanging over the toilet – print of course – woman coming
out of a shell. There's the Warhol in here if you like that
postmodern thing and if you look out the window, there's a
field with two cows and a sign saying 'Fresh eggs'. They
don't know what they want, so they want it every way.

EVE. Well, it's only open a week. It's had very good write-ups.

PATRICK. Is that why you picked it?

EVE. No.

PATRICK. Why did you pick it?

EVE. Because it's closer to Meath than to Dublin.

PATRICK. And you – live in Dublin?

EVE *smiles and takes out a small pile of magazines.*

EVE. I brought some magazines.

PATRICK *looks at her blankly.*

PATRICK. Magazines?

EVE. I thought it might help, you know – get things going.

PATRICK. Right. Sorry. I thought you meant – I thought for a
second you got them from reception.

EVE. Oh. No. I doubt they sell these at reception.

PATRICK. No. Because they're…

EVE. Yeah.

PATRICK. Not country walks.

EVE. No, not country walks.

PATRICK. Naked women?

EVE. Mostly.

PATRICK. Just checking.

EVE. You do – like women?

PATRICK. Certainly. I like them nearly as much as country walks.

EVE. It's just people's tastes around these things are – I've never really explored this whole territory in much detail so I thought I should get a few options because I didn't really know – I mean we never really got into that in the emails, did we?

PATRICK. No, we didn't.

He sips his drink. She looks at the magazines.

EVE. Man in Easons gave me the strangest look when I brought these to the counter.

PATRICK. It was probably admiration.

EVE. I don't think so. I was as red.

EVE *opens one of the magazines and starts flipping through in an effort to be casual.*

All the girls in this one are supposed to be a size ten and have behaved very poorly in school it seems, so they're in need of a good sorting out. And I think they get it on page fifteen, so... .

PATRICK. I see.

She quickly moves onto another magazine.

EVE. In this one, from what I gather, the girls mainly like other girls, but they're also quite fond of other men joining in at opportune moments. (*Showing him a picture.*) Like that one. And they seem to be fairly indiscriminate about what those men look like so – I'll leave that with you.

PATRICK *takes the second magazine tentatively.* EVE *opens a third.*

Now this one is a sort of specialist one. From France. Bit out of left field. The women don't tend to shave. As you can see.

PATRICK. Maybe we could do this later.

EVE. What?

PATRICK. Maybe we could – look at these later. It's sort of…
    putting me off.

EVE. Oh. (*Thinks he's referring to the pictures*.) The French
    don't seem to mind about underarm hair, but if it's not your
    cup of tea –

PATRICK. Not the hair. It's not the – I just don't feel quite
    there, yet. You know.

EVE. Oh. God, sorry. I – I wasn't trying to rush you.

PATRICK. It's fine.

EVE. I just – wanted you to know that I had them. If needs be.

PATRICK. Very kind.

    She puts the magazines down quickly.

EVE. I could go back out for a bit.

PATRICK. No. No. You don't need to do that. I had just hoped
    that we might – ease our way into this a bit more, you know.
    Take our time before we –

EVE. Of course. Well –

PATRICK. Maybe you'd tell me your name?

EVE. I'm not sure that's a very good idea.

PATRICK. Well, it isn't 'Annie 27' I know that.

EVE. No, it isn't but –

PATRICK. My name's Patrick. In the real world. When I'm not
    behind a computer screen chatting to women I've never met.
    I'm Patrick.

EVE. Okay.

PATRICK. You'll see it anyway, it's on the medical cert.
    (*Reaches into his pocket and takes out a piece of paper.*)
    Here. There's my address top of the page.

EVE (*taking it*). Right.

PATRICK. They gave me the all-clear in everything, see?

EVE (*reading*). Yes.

PATRICK. So nothing to be worrying about there then.

EVE. No. Look, I'm sorry you had to go to all this /

PATRICK. No trouble. I was relieved myself truth be told. Never been one for doctors – it was a good excuse for a thorough investigation.

EVE. Well, thank you –

PATRICK. Patrick.

EVE. I appreciate it. I just wanted to make sure everything was –

PATRICK. Good to go? It is. I am. You have it there in writing from St James'.

She folds the medical certificate and puts it away.

So, do I get a name or do I have to go home empty-handed?

EVE *looks at him and relents.*

EVE. My name's… Colette.

PATRICK. Colette?

EVE. That's right.

PATRICK. Are you serious?

EVE. Yes.

He stands back, assessing her.

PATRICK. Colette. God. I wouldn't have said that.

EVE. Why not?

PATRICK. I don't know. You don't seem much like a Colette.

EVE. Do you know many Colettes?

PATRICK. I have come across one or two in my time yes.

EVE. And what were they like?

PATRICK. Both very attractive.

EVE. I see.

PATRICK. Not that you're not. Jesus, I didn't mean that but – you know. It just doesn't. The way you're dressed. I would have figured you for more of a – Bernie or something.

EVE. Bernie?

PATRICK. Yeah, Bernadette.

EVE. Bernadette!

PATRICK. I know it sounds a bit severe, but I've only ever had good experiences with Bernadettes. You know where you are with them. Good, capable sorts, Bernadettes. Solid hands. The sort of women who know how to tie a tight bandage.

EVE. There is absolutely nothing sexy about the name Bernadette.

PATRICK. Is it sexy you're trying to be?

EVE. No.

PATRICK. Do you think Colette's sexy?

EVE. No. It just sounds a bit exotic.

PATRICK. It's not you though is it?

EVE. Look – Patrick – I think that the less information /

PATRICK. I know.

EVE. Aside from the strictly /

PATRICK. I hear you.

EVE. I'm not trying to be difficult. It's just easier if we don't /

PATRICK. I understand, it's fine. Fine.

Beat.

Can I call you Bernadette?

EVE. For God's sake.

PATRICK. Colette's not right.

EVE. Look my name's Eve, alright.

PATRICK. Eve.

EVE. Yes.

PATRICK. It is, isn't it?

EVE. Yes.

PATRICK. Eve.

EVE. *Eve*.

PATRICK. Biblical.

EVE. Apparently.

PATRICK. Suits you. I once knew a girl called Eden.

EVE. Did you?

PATRICK. Yeah, American girl. Desperately allergic to shellfish. One prawn and she was dead as a doornail. So she said. I was never sure if it was true, or if she was just being dramatic but I was often tempted to slip one past her. Just to see what'd happen. It's awful how easily we go over to the dark side isn't it?

EVE. Hmmmmmn.

PATRICK. I mean I was only young but, I was in love with her. Imagine. Madly in love and still I was curious to see how she'd react to a clam. Are you a businesswoman, Eve?

EVE. Sorry?

PATRICK. What line of work are you in? Or is that too much information too?

EVE. I'm – yes, I'm in business.

PATRICK. That's what you said in the emails, but I wasn't sure if it was /

EVE. It's true.

PATRICK. Do you work for a company?

EVE. No, I work for myself.

PATRICK. Course you do. I work for myself too.

EVE. I know.

EVE gets up, visibly frustrated. She goes to her bag and starts looking through.

PATRICK. I won't ask what line of business.

EVE. I appreciate it.

PATRICK. Though I have a feeling it's sales. You'd be good at sales. I'd say you're the persuasive type. You persuaded me in a couple of emails and that's not easy, I can tell you. I'm known for being a man who is not easily persuaded.

EVE. I brought a cup.

PATRICK. A cup?

EVE. Or a container. Whatever. For when you – I'm not trying to rush, but I just remembered and I thought I should say. It's here.

She holds up a plastic container for him to see.

PATRICK. Oh, right.

EVE. Do you want to have a look at it?

PATRICK. No, no you're grand.

EVE. Probably best. I had to sterilise it.

PATRICK. Ah.

EVE. You have to sterilise everything. I'll leave it by the sink in the bathroom. Okay?

PATRICK. Sure.

They look at one another for a beat before EVE *goes into the bathroom.*

EVE (*calling*). It's by the hot tap alright?

PATRICK (*calling back*). Great. I have my own company.

    EVE *comes back out*.

EVE. Sorry?

PATRICK. Property and all that, that's my line of things.

EVE. Oh.

 PATRICK. All gone to the dogs now o' course but once upon a time… sure people were hopping on that ladder like it was the bus into town.

EVE. Right.

    It's clear EVE *does not want to engage with this, but* PATRICK *keeps going*.

PATRICK.…It's hard working for yourself, don't you think?

EVE. Hmmmnnnn.

    She starts to busy herself again with things.

PATRICK. Tiring too – having to make decisions all the time.

EVE. Well, that gets easier as you get older. There's a lot less choice.

PATRICK. True. Though the hours are sort of getting to me now. Never used to mind them once upon a time. My wife – my ex-wife, we're separated – she used to say I was addicted to it. All the late nights. 'You can't take it with you.' She loved that expression.

EVE. And she was American?

PATRICK. No, no. Eden was American. The girl with the allergy? She wasn't my ex-wife.

EVE. Sorry. I got confused when you said you were in love with her.

PATRICK. Oh I *was* in love with her, with Eden. Not sure about the ex-wife though. It was sort of like a thirteen-year arm-wrestle, if you get me.

EVE. That's a pity.

PATRICK. What about you?

EVE. Me?

PATRICK. Any ex-husbands hanging around the periphery?

EVE. No. Nope.

PATRICK. Better off. Heartbreak can lead you to terrible things. Letter-writing.

EVE. How long more do you think you'll need?

PATRICK. Sorry?

EVE. I just – I worry that maybe we're losing focus here.

PATRICK. We're having a chat.

EVE. Would you like me to bring the cup into this room? Put it by the bed maybe.

PATRICK. You can leave it in the bathroom.

EVE. It's just – you didn't seem to like the bathroom.

PATRICK. I didn't not like the bathroom.

EVE. You said it was confused.

PATRICK. I said the decor was confused.

EVE. I'm just wondering if maybe you're uncomfortable going into the bathroom.

PATRICK. I've no problem with the bathroom.

EVE. But maybe the bathroom is the wrong place for the cup. And I was thinking – perhaps – that I should just bring the cup in here and then you know – I could go and order some tea in the lobby and take the brochure or whatever and – you could have some time to – relax.

PATRICK. With the magazines?

EVE. If you like.

PATRICK. And the cup?

EVE. Hmmmnnn.

PATRICK. I think I'd prefer it if you took the magazines. I could have a flick of the brochure.

EVE. If that's what floats your boat.

PATRICK. It isn't. I mean I don't know what floats my – I hope it is a floating boat. It *is*, generally but – (*Suddenly pointing to the weekend bag.*) Have you got some sort of a kit in there or something?

EVE. A kit?

PATRICK. In the bag. You keep taking things out of it – cups, magazines – and I was just wondering if you had some sort of kit for... doing the job.

EVE. Oh. Well, yes. I suppose I do have a kit. Sort of.

PATRICK. So is that cup in the bathroom – a special cup or something?

EVE. In a way. It has a wide rim apparently. For catching. You know.

PATRICK. Right.

She reaches into the bag and takes out the rest of the kit.

EVE. There's also a syringe – for collecting the fluid and a catheter for insertion. See?

PATRICK. I see.

He takes the syringe and catheter from her, looking at each closely.

EVE. They make it easy, really. It's weird to think that that's all it takes.

PATRICK. Well, it's not all it takes, but it's one option. So where does one pick up a package like this? Are they doing them in Arnotts now or –

EVE. I got it on eBay.

PATRICK. Oh.

EVE. There's a woman on it who sells the whole lot. Magic of the internet.

PATRICK. Magic.

PATRICK sits down on the bed slowly. He stares at the empty syringe.

EVE. So. Do you want me to get you the cup or –

PATRICK. This isn't very romantic is it?

EVE. What?

PATRICK. This. It isn't very romantic.

EVE. I didn't know it was meant to be romantic.

PATRICK. What's it meant to be?

EVE. Simple, I think. (*Beat.*) I'll get the cup.

She starts towards the bathroom.

PATRICK. No don't get the cup. I don't think I can face the cup just now.

She stops.

EVE. Are you – feeling alright, Patrick?

PATRICK. Yeah. Why? Do I not look alright?

EVE. You look fine. I just wondered if you were fine. Are you fine?

PATRICK. Yeah. I'm fine. I mean – there was this thing. Before. When I was on my way here in the car. I – well, I had this feeling you know. I had this feeling that I was – well, really looking forward to meeting you. In the flesh. It was sort of strange.

EVE. Well, I was looking forward to meeting you in the flesh too.

PATRICK. Yeah, but I found it hard to concentrate. You know, in work this morning and then on the drive here. I kept thinking about your profile on the website. I kept thinking about the things you wrote, about the sort of books you liked reading. And the sort of food you enjoyed and I got a bit excited because I thought – you know – I thought those are the sort of things I like too.

EVE. I think I said I liked Italian food and I read travel books.

PATRICK. Yeah you did.

EVE. Everybody likes Italian food.

PATRICK. So?

EVE. So, I just don't see what's so special about what I wrote.

PATRICK. There's nothing special about it. I just liked it, that's all. And I liked your picture.

EVE. I liked your picture too.

PATRICK. Yeah but – I liked it more than I liked the other women's pictures. I thought you were very pretty. You *are* very pretty.

EVE. Thank you.

PATRICK. And I thought – I *think* – that you have lovely kind eyes.

EVE. That's very nice of you to say.

PATRICK. And I thought you had great pair o' legs in that photo you had where you were dancing on the table. You looked a bit pissed, but you looked like the sort of girl who might be a bit of fun.

EVE. Well, I am a bit of fun, I suppose, when I'm myself.

PATRICK. See *that's* what I don't quite understand. You want me to have a child with you, but you don't want me to know anything about you and it seems... well, it seems a little brutal if you don't mind me saying.

EVE. Excuse me?

PATRICK. All this. It seems a bit unnecessarily cruel. I mean, I'm a pretty accommodating person, Eve. I was minding my own business on that website. I'd put my best picture up and I was chatting to some nice ladies. I'd even had dinner with some of them and I might have even been to bed with one or two because – I don't like to disappoint. But then you came along and you explained your situation and I thought okay, fair enough, that's very admirable and she's on her own and what's it going to cost me. But, now I'm here with you and Andy Warhol and I'm sort of wondering, you know.

EVE. Wondering what?

PATRICK. You're not very accessible.

EVE. Pardon?

PATRICK. You're a bit distant. How do I know you're going to be a good mother?

EVE. What?

PATRICK. I don't want to just hand my sperm out to anyone. I mean it's *my* sperm. It might not look like much sitting in a plastic cup but we're talking about a kid. I don't know anything about you. How do I know you're going to give that child everything it needs?

EVE. Look, Patrick /

PATRICK. What about schools? What about languages?

EVE. Languages?

PATRICK. In this day and age children should be bilingual. It's the future. We're behind the times here. Fourteen years of school Irish and most of us can't even say – *is maith liom an madra?* Is that even a sentence? I don't know if I want to have a child with a woman who isn't capable of love.

EVE. Who said I'm not capable of love?

PATRICK. Well, you're on your own aren't you?

EVE. That has nothing to do with being incapable of love and for the record I'm not having a child *with* you, I'm having a child by myself and you are for all intents and purposes, a donor. That's the situation here, Patrick. That's what you agreed to.

PATRICK. I know that's what I agreed but –

EVE. But what?

PATRICK. What do your family think about this?

EVE. That's none of your business.

PATRICK. They must have some opinion. You said in the emails you had three sisters? Do they know what you're doing in this hotel room with me?

EVE. I don't have to answer this.

PATRICK. Why did you want to meet me then? I could have just taken a sample and sent it in the post.

EVE. I wanted to meet you because I wanted to get a sense of the sort of person you are.

PATRICK. And here am I trying to tell you.

EVE. In your emails and on the phone, Patrick, you seemed like a very – together man.

PATRICK. I am a very together man.

EVE. And a man is what I wanted. Look, most sperm donors are twenty-one-year-olds looking for a way to make some quick cash. A lot of them are students. Apparently, many come from Denmark – not that I have anything against the Danes – but I just thought it would be nicer to actually *see* the man who was going to gift me his genes. I thought it would be somewhat more comforting to have a face to remember when I… The idea of going to the nearest sperm bank and picking an anonymous glass jar and saying 'cheers' just didn't seem to me to be wholly satisfactory.

PATRICK. It isn't wholly satisfactory.

EVE. Which is why I asked to meet you. Look, Patrick. I thought I'd made this very clear. You are under no obligation to me. After today –

PATRICK. Can I take you to dinner?

EVE. Pardon?

PATRICK. I know a great Italian in town. We could drive there now. We haven't been here two minutes really. They probably won't even charge us.

EVE. You can't be serious.

PATRICK. They'll probably feel sorry for you. They'll think I couldn't get it up and after all your wantonness – it was all a bit of a let-down.

EVE. We can't go for dinner, Patrick.

PATRICK. If you knew me out there in the real world. If you saw me with my clients I think you'd be very impressed.

EVE. I'm sure I would but the fact is –

PATRICK. The fact is there's something lonely about a woman in a hotel room with a plastic cup and catheter. And personally, I can't bear it. Please let me take you out.

Beat.

EVE. I've heard about this.

PATRICK. You've heard about what?

EVE. This. What you're doing now.

PATRICK. I'm asking you to dinner.

EVE. No you're not. You might think you're asking me to dinner, but you're not.

PATRICK. What am I doing then?

EVE. There's reasons sperm banks don't take donations from men your age, Patrick. Risk of low sperm count is one obvious one, but it has been noted that older men tend to get too involved. They don't seem to accept that after ejaculation their work is done, they start asking questions and interfering, wanting to meet the mothers.

PATRICK. Well, what's so wrong with that?

EVE. They're unreliable in their anonymity.

PATRICK. They're probably just trying to be decent people.

EVE. It's selfish.

PATRICK. How is it any more selfish than what you're doing? Older men have been around, they know about the knocks a kid can have.

EVE. They're not wanted.

Beat.

Why don't you have any children of your own, Patrick?

PATRICK. What?

EVE. Thirteen years is a long time to be married, surely it crossed your minds.

PATRICK. Yeah. We didn't want them.

EVE. You didn't want children?

PATRICK. No. Well. We couldn't have them. My wife had a problem with her – Couldn't hold onto the embryo or something they said. Kept miscarrying, so we stopped.

EVE. You just stopped?

PATRICK. Well, of course we stopped. You don't need to see someone go through that ten times to know it isn't doing them any good. She was a wreck. Anyway, the way things turned out it was a probably a blessing, wasn't it?

EVE. You're not going to be the only sperm donor, Patrick. I think I should tell you that right now, straight up. Just in case you have some – idea or other about this being an opportunity to – it isn't. You're not. There are two other men donating too.

PATRICK. What do you mean… 'two other men'?

EVE. I mean there are two other men who will meet me in a hotel room much like this one and give me a cup of their sperm.

PATRICK.…Why?

EVE. Because. I'm not exactly a nubile nymphet in case you haven't noticed. At my age something like this doesn't just work the first time. I have to have options. You won't be the only one. I think you should know that.

PATRICK. So, what? You met these other men on the internet too?

EVE. One of them, yes.

PATRICK. And what about the other?

EVE. The other's from Poland.

PATRICK. Poland?

EVE. Yes. He's in his twenties so he's –

PATRICK. Virile.

EVE. Yes.

PATRICK. I see. And where did you stumble across this virile Pole?

EVE. He tiled my sister's bathroom.

PATRICK. Bathroom. Nice. So you're basically screwing the help?

EVE. I'm not screwing anyone, Patrick. I'm tired of being screwed, that's the point.

PATRICK. To be honest, I don't see any point. I think you'd be better off with your glass jar full of stranger than this.

EVE. Well, forgive me for wanting a human encounter.

PATRICK. Is that what this is?

Silence. They both seem a little shaken.

EVE. Look. I'm glad actually, that we've had this time. That we've had this little – talk because it's quite clear that this isn't the right thing for you, Patrick. Not now. And I wouldn't ever want to put anybody into a position that they didn't want to be in. I thought we had an understanding. I thought I'd been very plain about this whole business and I have done a *lot* of research but somewhere along the way we've – gotten our wires crossed. And that's okay because, now they're uncrossed. Now we know where we stand and – I don't think we stand in the same place. So… I think maybe, you and I should probably just call it a day, Patrick, alright?

PATRICK *sits, silent.*

Yeah, I think that's probably the right thing to do. I'm sorry if this hasn't turned out the way you hoped, but… things often don't. Believe me.

PATRICK. When you came in here earlier on, you made that joke. About me still having my clothes on and you not being Mae West or something. It went a bit over my head to be honest, but still I thought fair play to you, you know, for trying. I like tryers. I'd like to think I was a tryer.

EVE. Well, sometimes it's important to know when to stop.

PATRICK. True. My wife left me in the end because she wanted to stop. Trying. It was the right thing to do but I couldn't bring myself to it. I hated the thought of breaking the promise.What have you got if not your own word?

Slowly he picks up one of the magazines that EVE *had left down earlier.*

Is this the one with the hairy birds?

EVE. I think so. Look, Patrick, I think we should just quit while we're ahead here.

PATRICK. No. We just shouldn't have got talking like that. You were right. I got distracted. I came here to do something and I'm going to do it. Don't worry.

EVE. I don't think you're in any frame of mind /

PATRICK. I'm not the sort of man who lets people down. I'm a
    lot of other things but I'm not that. And you *were* crystal
    clear from the beginning about this whole – situation. It's
    none of my business why you're doing it or who you're
    doing it with. I just – I saw you get out of your car today
    with your little suitcase and your hair all nice and that skirt
    and I thought… well, I suppose I thought that no one should
    have to be that brave on their own. But Jesus. Who am I to
    pass judgement on someone else's life?

He looks at the magazine.

Bear with me on this. Won't be too long I hope.

He goes into the bathroom.

EVE. Patrick –

PATRICK *shuts the door.*

Patrick!

PATRICK. I'll probably need a few minutes.

EVE. But…

EVE *stands outside the door for a few seconds at a loss.*

Fuck.

*She paces for a moment, then goes to the bed and sits down.
She picks up one of the magazines, makes a face and puts it
down again. She stands up, tense, and strides over to the
bathroom door. She is about to knock but doesn't instead she
whispers:*

Shit.

*Maybe she goes to the mini-bar and pours herself a drink,
something to steady her nerves. Cautiously, she moves back
to the bathroom door and listens.*

Are you… are you alright in there, Patrick?

PATRICK (*calling*). Fine thanks, Eve.

Beat. She listens again.

EVE. You're not – upset or anything, are you?

PATRICK (*strained*). No.

EVE. Because you know, I'm sorry if some of the things I said
before were a bit – or if any of the questions, you know,
about your – marriage, seemed sort of invasive.

Silence.

It sounds like you've been through quite a lot.

Silence.

I think it's a shame that things didn't work out for you with
your wife, I really do. Or with that girl with the shellfish
allergy. It's never easy, but, you know, maybe feeling pain is
better than feeling nothing at all.

She makes a face wondering if she's saying the wrong thing.

I wasn't – meaning to be cold earlier on. I was trying to do
things by the book. Not that there is a book on this sort of
thing. Well, there are lots of books actually, but you know
what I mean… I always hoped that I'd be in a hotel room
like this with a man. With a real man. Of course you *are* a
real man, but a man who I was in love with, you know. Not
that there's anything wrong with being here with a cup and a
catheter by the way. I don't agree with you about that. It
might seem sad to some people but I actually think we're
lucky to live in an age where women like me have that
choice. I suppose men don't have a choice yet do they? A
man wanting to conceive a child on his own, I don't know
how people would react to that, but you never know. Some
day. Modern technology.

Beat.

It's funny because in England there's this whole shortage of
sperm right now. They're practically begging guys to give it
away because they changed the law, so children of donors
can trace their fathers now. And most men don't want that,
obviously. *Most* men find that a horrifying prospect. Yeah.

She paces.

My sisters don't know that I'm here. With you. They're
married, all three of them. One of them works. Well, I say
she works, she makes these little porcelain animals – pigs
and goats and stuff and her friend sells them in her shop – so
it's not really a job job. I'm the one with the great career.
That's what they like to say, 'You're the one with the great
career.' That's sort of a code for saying I haven't got a
boyfriend. Which is sort of a code for saying I'm weird.
They try to be nice.

They used to do a lot of breastfeeding, my sisters. They used
to do a lot of talking about breastfeeding too. And actually
for a long time I thought that the three of them had been
mentally retarded by childbirth because they couldn't seem
to talk about anything else. But now I see it was just because
it was all so very consuming. Which is what love is, isn't it?

She listens for a response.

I don't think I'd want them to know about this. I'm not
ashamed. I just – think they'd feel better if they thought I got
drunk and shagged a stranger. Much more natural.

Beat.

You were wrong about me being in sales by the way. And
you were wrong about my persuasive skills. But it was nice
of you to say.

She drinks. She leans against the door tenderly.

I have been in hotel rooms like this before with men that I've
loved. At the time. I'm sure you must have been in hotels
with women that you loved too – your ex-wife or… Eden.
It's been a while. I can't remember what it felt like really but
I must have felt smug. You must feel smug being in love.
You must feel that at long last you're finally doing something
right because – well, because you matter to someone else.
You're important to someone else. It's not just – you. Who
wouldn't want that?

A toilet flushes. The sound of PATRICK *coughing.* EVE *steps
back and tries to gather herself.* PATRICK *opens the door.
He is holding the magazine.*

PATRICK. Hello.

EVE. Hi. Hi. Did you – get on okay?

PATRICK. Grand thanks. (*Beat*.) Took a bit of concentration.

EVE. Sorry. Yeah I – sorry.

PATRICK. It's alright. The end was as predicted, thank God.

EVE. Good.

PATRICK. That's the thing about ageing, you don't get any faster in any department.

EVE *looks at the magazine in* PATRICK*'s hand*.

EVE. No. Do you want me to – take that?

PATRICK. No, sure I'll hang on to it. I'm sort of fond of them now actually. My furry friends.

He smiles. She smiles too. He steps into the room.

EVE. Okay.

PATRICK. Okay. Well, I'm starving.

EVE. Yes, you must be.

PATRICK. You staying here tonight then? In the – Serenity Room?

EVE. Probably. I think so. Yeah.

PATRICK. You don't mind being by yourself?

EVE. I quite like it actually. I won't always be able to afford the luxury.

PATRICK. No sure, in a year's time you'll probably be grateful for a night's sleep.

EVE. Yeah.

A beat.

PATRICK *begins shifting towards the door.*

PATRICK. Well, I should really make a – Apparently I have a train to catch.

EVE *laughs nervously.*

How long do you have? You know, to use it?

EVE. About half an hour.

PATRICK. Is that all?

EVE. After that it starts… dying.

PATRICK. Right. Right. Well… Do you think you will? Use it? Or did I ruin everything with my shenanigans earlier?

EVE. I'm not sure yet.

PATRICK. I shouldn't have opened my big trap should I?

EVE. I'll just have to have a think you know.

PATRICK. Sure. Sure. Have a think. Have a cup of tea, see how you feel. Well. It was nice to meet you anyway, Eve. In the flesh.

EVE. It was nice to meet you too, Patrick

PATRICK. And I hope it all goes well for you with the – Pole and the other fella. Should be a doddle. First one's always the worst, isn't that what they say?

EVE. I don't know… what they say.

He nods and moves to the door, opening it with one hand. He stops.

PATRICK Well. Cup's on the sink by the way. By the hot tap. Just in case you're looking.

EVE. Thanks.

PATRICK. No worries.

He closes the door. EVE *sits down on the bed and looks towards the bathroom.*

Lights down.

MEETING MISS IRELAND

Rosemary Jenkinson

ROSEMARY JENKINSON

Rosemary Jenkinson was born in Belfast in 1967. Her collection of short stories, *Contemporary Problems Nos. 53 & 54*, was published by Lagan Press in 2004, while her first play, *The Bonefire*, produced by Rough Magic, was published by Methuen in 2006 and won the Stewart Parker BBC Radio Drama Award. Other plays include *The Winners* (Ransom); *Johnny Meister and the Stitch* (Jigsaw, Belfast/Edinburgh Fringe/Dublin Fringe/Solas Nua, Washington DC); *Bruised* (Tinderbox); *The Lemon Tree* (Origin, New York as part of the 1st Irish Festival); and *1 in 5* (Kabosh). Her short-play commission *Meeting Miss Ireland* was presented as part of The Fairer Sex series of readings on the Peacock stage in 2009. She has had three plays, *Stella Morgan*, *Basra Boy* and *Cuchullain*, produced by the Keegan Theatre in Washington DC, and *Basra Boy* was subsequently revived by Brassneck at the Féile an Phobail and East Belfast Arts Festival in 2012. Also in 2012, *White Star of the North* was produced by the Lyric Theatre as part of the Titanic commemorations and *Ghosts of Drumglass* was performed by Kabosh in the Belfast Festival. Her radio play, *Castlereagh to Kandahar*, was broadcast on BBC3's The Wire. She took part in the BBC College of Comedy and was writer-on-attachment at the National Theatre Studio in 2010.

Meeting Miss Ireland was first performed as a rehearsed reading as part of The Fairer Sex play-reading series for the Abbey Theatre, Dublin, in 2009. The cast was as follows:

KATHY IRELAND	Karen Ardiff
STEVIE IRELAND	Karl Shiels
Director	Wayne Jordan

Characters

KATHY IRELAND, *thirty-seven*
STEVIE IRELAND, *thirty-four*

Scene One

A living room. Belfast.

KATHY *is sitting expectantly at a small table, wearing a sticker that says 'Kathy 1'. She has a form and a pencil in front of her. She has made a great effort to dress up and looks stunning.*

The door opens and STEVIE *comes in confidently. He is wearing a sticker that says 'George 2'.*

KATHY. Hello!

STEVIE. Hello yourself there.

KATHY (*looking at his name badge*). So, you're George.

STEVIE (*sitting down*). And you must be Katie.

KATHY. Kathy.

STEVIE. Kathy.

KATHY. And you're number two. (*Writes it down.*) So, here we are, George.

STEVIE. Here we are indeed.

KATHY. Isn't it swish?

STEVIE (*looks around him*). Very salubrious.

KATHY. So what do you do of an evening... normally?

STEVIE. Well, normally. (*Thinks.*) That's a good question. A very good question.

KATHY. I know. Pertinent.

STEVIE. Well, normal... I like watching the documentaries.

KATHY (*delightedly*). Oh!

STEVIE. Yes, there was one last night on about chimpanzees.

KATHY. I love chimpanzees. I love the way you call them chimpanzees and not chimps.

STEVIE. Well, you have to accord them with their full title, don't you? Yes, well, it was all about them grooming each other for hours. See, with them, it's a form of foreplay.

KATHY (*biting her pen top*). That is fascinating.

STEVIE. It is.

KATHY. Animals and their lives. What job is it you do, George?

STEVIE. Well, at the current moment in time I sell drugs.

KATHY. Oh, the pharmaceutical industry, how wonderful.

STEVIE. No, I sell a bit of the G. The marijuana, like.

KATHY. Is that rewarding?

STEVIE. Yes. Yes, it is, Kathy. Because I sell medicinally only. To people who have the rheumatism.

KATHY (*writing*). That's kind.

STEVIE. And of course I'm also primary carer of me sister who's mentally impaired.

KATHY. You fucking shut it now.

STEVIE. What?

KATHY. You fucking wee shite.

STEVIE. What?

KATHY. You're meant to make something up, aren't you?

STEVIE. Here, what were you writing about us?

KATHY (*withholds her form*). It's *my* notes.

STEVIE (*grabs it off her, reads*). Bullshitter, am I!

KATHY. Well, boy, if you only sell to the rheumatic, then there's a powerful lot of people crippled with it round here is all I'm saying. Besides, Stevie, you can't be selling drugs cos this is role-play. (*Points at his sticker.*) You're George.

STEVIE. God, but I am sick of this.

KATHY. Please. (*Looking at her watch.*) In one hour's time I'll be at the Wellington Park Hotel.

STEVIE. I'm not equipped.

KATHY. You're a man.

STEVIE. I'm your brother.

KATHY. You're still a man.

STEVIE. Real men don't do role-play.

KATHY. Please, Stevie. Ask *me* some questions this time. Prepare me. I've never done speed-dating before. This is important.

STEVIE *sighs*.

Wait – I'll cook you a breakfast all next week.

STEVIE (*considers*). Hmm. Alright.

KATHY. Great. Thank you. Now you be Leonardo this time.

She sticks the name sticker on him: 'Leonardo 3'.

STEVIE. Leonardo?

KATHY. That's right.

STEVIE. Wait – as in DiCaprio?

KATHY. Well, he was only a loose inspiration behind the name.

STEVIE. Wait. (*Catching on.*) Was I meant to be George Clooney just there?

KATHY. Yes. (*Shows him the next sticker.*) Brad's waiting in the wings too. It helps me... visually.

STEVIE. Fuck sake.

KATHY. Now hurry! Out you go and come back in a tick.

STEVIE *exits*.

KATHY *moves the table, unable to decide where it should best go. She suddenly spots something through the window. She leaps up and yells. She picks up a pump-action water gun and rushes to the window, opening it and squirting out jets of water.*

STEVIE *comes back in*.

Wee bastard.

STEVIE. Is he back?

KATHY. Wee bullying bastard sitting on our front wall.

STEVIE. You used to love robins.

KATHY. They peck at the other birds all day. I read about them in the paper. Nasty wee faces.

STEVIE. Now can we go back to the job?

KATHY *suddenly waves at someone out the window*.

KATHY. There's that lovely old Stuart.

STEVIE. Who?

KATHY. I love old people – they make me feel young! Of course that's not their only function in life. Stuart. Hasn't he a beautiful white moustache. If I slept with him, I'd call him Snowy.

STEVIE. Are we doing this or what?

KATHY. Of course. (*Waves him out the door.*) Back you go.

STEVIE *goes out again*.

KATHY *prepares herself, pushes her hair back*.

STEVIE *breezes back in confidently*.

Hello there!

STEVIE. Hello there – (*Reads her sticker.*) Kathy, how are you?

KATHY. Oh, I'm lovely, you?

STEVIE (*sitting down*). You *are* lovely.

KATHY. Why, thank you, Leonardo.

STEVIE (*claps his hands together*). Now, girl, we only have five minutes chatting time here, so let's cut to the meat and bone of it. Why are you here tonight?

KATHY. Well, I'm looking to meet men.

STEVIE. Good. Honesty is good.

KATHY. I go to the church, see, but they're all awful old. Halfway to Heaven already.

STEVIE. So how old would you be yourself?

KATHY. Well...

STEVIE. If it's not rude.

KATHY. My actual age is twenty-nine.

STEVIE. Actual?

KATHY. Well. My real age is thirty-seven but you can subtract a few years for not smoking and for eating healthy. I done it last week in a magazine.

STEVIE. You certainly are looking well on it for your years.

KATHY. Oh, I like to look after myself. See, in a manner of speaking I'm Miss Ireland. My full name is Kathy Ireland. Well, Katherine Ireland. Katherine Jane Ireland.

STEVIE. For pity fucking sake.

KATHY. If you was really a speed-dater you'd be interested.

STEVIE. Sorry. Go on.

KATHY. Miss Ireland. See, it sounds like a beauty queen, don'tn't it?

STEVIE. Aye. Right enough you've a lot to live up to.

KATHY. Can I be honest?

STEVIE. Fire away.

KATHY. I used to purge. It was a form of staying slim. It's that what I attribute my body to today.

STEVIE (*getting up*). Quit that! Just...

KATHY. What?

STEVIE. 'Purging.' You can't be spewing all that out on a first date.

KATHY. Was it a bit much?

STEVIE. They'll think you're off your wagon!

KATHY. God, I'm just so nervous.

STEVIE. I know you are but... do you want a wee dose of the sniffables?

KATHY. No!

STEVIE. To settle you.

KATHY. No!

STEVIE. Don't bite the head off us, well.

KATHY. Sorry. I'm just so... (*Opens her compact.*) How do I look?

STEVIE. Perfect, Kathy. I told you.

KATHY. My face needs a bit more colour.

STEVIE. Fuck sake, go and stick it under the grill then.

KATHY. You don't understand.

STEVIE (*takes a big bag of grass out of the sideboard*). Just crack on with it.

KATHY. But am I good enough for the Wellington Park? It's so... that word.

STEVIE. Salubrious.

KATHY. Salubrious. I want to make a lifestyle change. Before I'm forty. After forty you don't get no one.

STEVIE *sits down on the sofa. He starts to weigh out the grass on a set of scales sitting on the coffee table and put it into much smaller bags.*

To think I used to be a man-eater. Now it's not so much as a nibble. Not even a suck. All in four years I had was a holiday romance.

STEVIE. 'Holiday romance'! It was a day trip to Bangor.

KATHY. He was Turkish.

STEVIE. Holiday romance. You were kebabed by a Turkish kebab-turner.

KATHY. He was beautiful. Don't hurt me.

STEVIE. You hurt yourself.

KATHY. You don't want me to get anyone.

STEVIE. Crack on with it then.

KATHY. You don't want to be turfed out, that's your worry.

STEVIE *doesn't answer.*

You and your marijuana plants. They play havoc with my electric meter.

STEVIE. I pay for them, don't I?

KATHY. Less now than before.

STEVIE. Well, yes. The G is a luxury item, that's true. But way I look at it, a wee smoke helps get you through the credit crunch, helps numb you, like, there's always demand.

KATHY. Oh, give over. That's a year since you was burnt out of your last place and you're still here. No thought that I might get burnt out too.

STEVIE. All that biz is finished.

KATHY. You still get threats.

STEVIE. I tape up the letter box at night, don't I?

KATHY. Wowee!

STEVIE. I put a fire extinguisher in the hall, didn't I? Thanks to me, you're safer than ever before.

KATHY. I didn't have to be safe before, did I?

STEVIE falls silent.

KATHY looks out the window.

That rain doesn't know whether to be on or off. Me dress'll wilt. (*Adjusts it.*) It's not too unrevealing, is it? I've shaved special too.

STEVIE (*points to his lip*). You've missed a bit.

KATHY (*touches her legs*). Gillette. The best a man can get.

STEVIE. Fuck, but I do wish a man would come round and scalp you, so you'd give us some pace here.

KATHY. Oh, listen to himself sitting there splitting the atom.

STEVIE. I'm *working*.

KATHY. 'Working.' You don't even get up to twelve.

STEVIE. I'm saving on the heating! That's why. Alright?

KATHY. Aye, love. (*Sighs.*) I don't really blame you. Who'd want to get up with our weather?

She waves vigorously at someone out the window.

Shukran! Ihab Shoukri! Talibanski! Look, Stevie, it's that lovely Muslim girl in the burka.

STEVIE stands up to look.

Isn't she lovely? Shahid!

STEVIE (*strains to see*). How can you tell with her get-up?

KATHY. She has a lovely wee wave on her, but.

STEVIE. What was that you were shouting to her?

KATHY. Oh, just a bit of… Afghanish. It's amazing what you can pick up off the telly.

STEVIE, *disbelieving, goes back to bagging up his grass.*

She has a couple of sequins on her burka. Must be one of them racy ones, not that I'm one to judgement.

STEVIE. I heard tell her kids were out with our ones throwing stones at the Short Strand.

KATHY. Isn't it lovely they're integrating?

STEVIE. It's only fair. Sure the Catholics get all the Polish, so at least we're getting the Muslims. And the blacks.

KATHY. Oh, God, I'm so nervous. I know we've rehearsed but what if I pull a blank? (*Roots around in her handbag and pulls out an opened bag of mixed nuts.*) This'll work.

KATHY *starts eating them greedily.*

STEVIE. Christ, you'll bust out your dress in a sec.

KATHY. This is brain food.

STEVIE. It still goes straight onto your arse.

KATHY *sets down the nuts.*

KATHY. God, no, I'll get soaked. I'll have to take an umberella.

STEVIE. Sure I said I'd drive you.

KATHY. Will you, love?

STEVIE (*putting the big bag of grass in the sideboard*). Sure I've a couple of wee baggies to drop off. Are you right then?

KATHY. I'm just so het up.

STEVIE. You'll be grand, Kathy.

KATHY. Oh, I know. Mum used to say, what's for you won't go by you.

STEVIE. That fucking big bus didn't go by her anyway.

KATHY. Oh, don't bring that up tonight, Stevie.

STEVIE. Sorry, sorry. C'mon, well.

KATHY. Stevie. Am I alright?

STEVIE. Aye, but don't hold your bag there like a fucking sporran. Who'll want to scalp you like that?

KATHY. Do you think someone will?

STEVIE. Kathy. You look stunning.

KATHY. I don't know what I'll do if they ask. Sex isn't supposed to be easy. Sure God covered our wee button up so men couldn't find it.

STEVIE. For fuck sake. Get out into that fucking car, will you?

KATHY. Aye, love.

KATHY goes out.

STEVIE picks up the small bags of grass off the coffee table and pockets them.

(*Off.*) Stevie. Do I look big in this coat?

STEVIE shakes his head in long-suffering disbelief. He goes out.

Scene Two

Living room. STEVIE is sitting on the sofa. His mobile rings.

STEVIE (*answers*). 'Lo?

He listens.

Aye, very original. (*Listens some more.*) Look, you can't rip me intestine out and stuff it up me arse, it'd be too floppy. (*Listens.*) And I don't give a flying flute if you do chop me sister's arms off and spit in her stumps, cos she's a right pain in the fucking hole. Aye, yap away, son. (*Listens.*) Aye, well, you better not come here, for I'll...

The person who phoned him has hung up.

(*Hits the redial button, muttering to himself.*) I'm not finished with you, you… (*The person on the other end answers.*) Listen you up, you come here I'll fix your whack, I'll fucking tear… (*The mobile has gone dead, he presses redial again, but it doesn't work.*) Ah, no credit! Just when you fucking need it.

He marches to the sideboard and takes out a baseball bat.

He sits back down on the sofa with the baseball bat beside him. His right leg is jiggling with nerves.

The front door slams and STEVIE *jumps up.*

Kathy?

KATHY *comes in, almost waltzing.*

KATHY. Oh, Stevie.

STEVIE (*stashing the baseball bat down the side of the sofa*). God, you near gave us a heart attack.

KATHY. What a wondrous night!

STEVIE. But I thought I was picking you up.

KATHY. I got a lift. Off Lenny.

STEVIE. You said you'd phone. I thought you'd been kidnapped by some man.

KATHY. What a wonderful thought.

STEVIE. So it went alright then?

KATHY. Alright? It was… wondrous.

STEVIE *sits back down.*

STEVIE. Lenny. Who's that, like, Leonardo DiCaprio?

He laughs.

KATHY. You can laugh. He called me Miss Ireland all night.

STEVIE. I bet he did.

KATHY. He's beautiful. A big beautiful redhead.

STEVIE. You're kidding.

KATHY. Oh, I told him I was all for saving the ginger squirrels. He liked that. I told him I'd happily shoot them grey ones.

STEVIE. A fucking reddie but.

KATHY. After I'd shot the robins, like.

STEVIE. Kathy, nobody wants a ginger scrote in the family.

KATHY. Rubbish, he was telling us all the fringe benefits of ginger folk. Did you know, their skin produces high levels of vitamin D? I'd love to give our child a head-start.

STEVIE. You were talking about kids?

KATHY. Well, not quite yet.

STEVIE. Here, don't you think you're jumping the gun a bit?

KATHY. Oh, I'll be jumping his gun soon enough, boy.

STEVIE. For fuck sake, you don't even know him.

KATHY. You're not even glad for me, Stevie.

STEVIE. I am. It's just I don't want you took advantage of. Men, they just want somewhere warm to kip, see.

KATHY (*with irony*). So I've noticed. (*Pause.*) Well, you better pack up cos I can't be having you in the house when he's here.

STEVIE (*nearly speechless*). What?

KATHY. You, you cramp my style and my house.

STEVIE. You want me to go?

KATHY. Yes. As soon as you can, please.

STEVIE. But me plants. Sure they haven't reached maturity.

KATHY. Neither have you but you still have to go.

STEVIE. But, but you promised to cook me breakfast next week.

KATHY. End of next week then.

STEVIE. But… I've nowhere to go.

KATHY. The Welly Park. God, it's so salubrious.

STEVIE. You can't just jump this on us, Kathy.

KATHY. Five minutes is all it takes. Lifetimes are based on it.

STEVIE. Kathy. Are you drunk?

KATHY. I'm drunk on love!

STEVIE. And cocktails.

KATHY. And cocktails. I only had a couple. They gave us Buck's Fizz on arrival. (*Re: a fly.*) Oh, look at that! Look at its azure wings. It pure takes you to be in love to see it. (*Examining it up close.*) The light tracery. (*Pause.*) Like a lattice window. Miraculous.

STEVIE (*flaps at it*). It's only a fucking fly, you dingbat.

KATHY *goes and picks up the watergun.*

KATHY. Aye, it's a pity it has no thought of hygiene. He's a Catholic. I've always been so turned on by Catholics.

Squirt.

The idea of them confessing their sins to me.

Squirt. STEVIE *ducks.*

Got it! All them deathbed confessions, it's all beds and dark places with them, so sexy.

She shivers feverishly. Sits down next to STEVIE.

And he's so into us too. Did you know he has a thing for us whistling our flutes?

Pause.

STEVIE. Aye. Aye, I bet he has.

KATHY. And just what do you mean by that?

STEVIE. Sure he'll babe you up and bounce you out, Kathy, I can see it all.

KATHY (*leaps up*). Lenny would never.

STEVIE. Love, honey, you don't even know him.

KATHY. You're fucking jealous, that's it! Just cos you can't get a girl.

STEVIE. Can so!

KATHY. You have to spoil it every time, don't you? Sure the last man you chased off.

STEVIE. He was a peeler. He only came here to take a statement on me death threats.

KATHY. But I could have had something good with Mustafa.

STEVIE. Throwing yourself away on a Turkish delight. I saved you, sure.

KATHY (*spotting the baseball bat down the side of the sofa*). Excuse me, what's this?

KATHY *pulls the bat out.*

Oh, for fuck sake, Stevie.

STEVIE. Now don't be worrying.

KATHY. How? Sure the last time they burnt you out.

STEVIE. Look, nobody's doing pipe bombs any more.

KATHY. And the new sofa bought too.

STEVIE. Oh, that's very touching. And me about to be…

KATHY. Putting me in danger.

STEVIE. They never even mentioned you. You don't know what they'll do to me… Oh, God.

He clasps his head with his hands.

KATHY. Oh, love. Does it hurt?

STEVIE. Yes. Yes.

KATHY *starts to massage his head.*

KATHY. I didn't mean to upset you.

STEVIE. Well, I am upset. Them boys aren't joking.

KATHY. It's just my head is so full of Lenny. Who could have dreamt – is that good?

STEVIE. Yes.

KATHY. Oh, Stevie, I'm on a rocket to the moon!

The sound of a plane passing overhead.

STEVIE. Aye, that'll be him now come to whisk you off on his easyJet.

KATHY. Oh, I hope he'll take me on the big wheel at Christmas.

Pause. She pats her stomach.

I'm not even hungry any more.

STEVIE. Look at you standing there like a continental porn star.

KATHY. I'm just so thrilled! I told him I lived in the Titanic Quarter. He's very excited about living here.

STEVIE. You did this all in five minutes?

KATHY. Not at all, he stayed at my table the whole night. The organisers kept ringing the bell at us, but we only had ears for each other. Lenny was quite masterful over it. He said he'd paid his twenty pound and wasn't for budging. Oh, we talked of everything. Of my first love and how, God rest him, he was one of the Disappeared.

STEVIE. Aye, disappeared alright – over the hills, not under them.

KATHY. Don't be so cruel. He loved me. (*Spots* STEVIE*'s leg jiggling.*) What do you want to do, the Riverdance?

STEVIE. Look, I'm nervous, Kathy.

KATHY. It's your own fault for consorting with bad people. Oh, why didn't you stick to selling coke to the rich and famous?

STEVIE. I know.

KATHY. You had it made. Sure Jimmy Nesbitt was never done phoning of you at all hours.

She stops massaging his head.

Oh, and guess who was there tonight. A real blast from our past, Stevie.

STEVIE. Tell us.

KATHY. Julie-Ann Gibson!

STEVIE. Julie-Ann Gibson. Sure she should have got a man by now.

KATHY. Well, we all should have, Stevie. But you should see her now. All… (*Sucks in her cheeks.*)

STEVIE. Sure she was…

KATHY. Oh, aye. Miss Lodge Lovely 1990 she was. To think she was serenaded by a flute band, thought she was it. How she's faded!

KATHY *sits down next to him on the sofa.*

Look at me. Lenny told me my eyes shone like the stars. See? It's that new glittery mascara. I lathered it on, you can't bate it. Remember I did Mum's on her in the coffin? Oh, if she'd seen herself, she'd have wore make-up all the time.

STEVIE. I have to say she did look well on it.

KATHY. In spite of the bus.

STEVIE. In spite of the bus.

They muse.

KATHY. Mum would shudder to see you in trouble again.

STEVIE (*gets up*). Kathy, no.

KATHY. She was always for saying it was cos you were conceived under the UVF mural that made you so bad.

STEVIE. You quit it!

KATHY. Sorry.

STEVIE. You don't understand. Listen, I'm terrified!

KATHY. D'you want some seratonin?

STEVIE *shakes his head.*

It'll help you. (*Leaps up.*) I can't sit still even if it is terrible of me. Lenny, I love you!

She starts to whirl around and sing the chorus from 'Rule the World' by Take That.

STEVIE (*catches hold of her wrist to make her stop*). Kathy. I have nowhere else to go.

KATHY *sucks in her breath.*

KATHY. Look, Stevie.

She picks up a feather from the carpet.

A feather. It's a sign from a loved one.

STEVIE. It's from the cushion.

KATHY. It's white. From a nice bird. Not a robin. (*Holds it to her chest.*) I feel Mum, don't you?

STEVIE. It's weird but… (*Looks around him, feeling a strange sensation.*) Y'know, I feel Mum too.

KATHY. She always said if you talk of the dead, you raise them.

STEVIE. Oh, Mum. I didn't mean for Dad to be… I was only for looking at the arms dump, I was only a wee kid…

KATHY. Shh-shh. She says she'll protect you, Stevie. She says…

STEVIE *waits for* KATHY *to receive Mum's message.*

Find a girl she says.

STEVIE (*catching on*). Here, wait, there's no way I'm going speed-dating at the Welly Boot.

KATHY. Sure I'm an expert now, I can train you up.

STEVIE. I'm not that desperate!

KATHY. You are. You're near homeless. Go on, Stevie, think of a girl you like.

STEVIE. Here, plenty chicks are into us.

KATHY. I mean one that isn't in a drug-induced coma.

STEVIE. Alright. (*Pause.*) Victoria Beckham.

KATHY. What? She's the bride of Bobby Sands! She's a scrawn.

STEVIE. Look, I like her, so I'll have her!

KATHY. Alright, alright. Keep your crust on. (*Writes on the sticker.*) 'Vic-toria 1.'

STEVIE (*laughs*). You?

KATHY. It may be a slight stretch but… (*Slaps on the sticker and walks towards the door.*) Now you get at that table and I'll go… (*Spots someone through the window and waves.*) Hello! Shoukri! (*Stops.*) Oh, my God, no!

STEVIE. What?!

KATHY. It's not her in her burka. It's a man in a balaclava. Quick! Get back.

STEVIE (*dives for the baseball bat*). Oh, fuck, I'll have to use this.

KATHY. No, you won't. I'll go.

STEVIE (*catches her by the arm*). But what'll you say, Kathy?

KATHY. Perhaps he'll not be in the mood for violence.

STEVIE. Haven't you clocked the balaclava?

There is a loud banging on the front door.

No!

KATHY. Love, you hide. I'll say you're not here. I'll say you're with a girl. No, he'll never believe that, I'll say…

STEVIE. Go, just go!

KATHY *leaves.* STEVIE *dives behind the sofa. Then he sees the feather lying on the floor, crawls out and picks it up.*

He puts it to his cheek.

Oh, Mum.

KATHY *comes in.*

KATHY. Stevie? Stevie?

STEVIE (*leaps up*). Is he gone?

KATHY. Aye. For now.

STEVIE. Thank Christ! (*Hugging her.*) Didn't I know you'd sort it!

KATHY. He was all for barging in but I said you'd just nipped out.

STEVIE. Good girl yourself.

KATHY. Right, let's go up and get your wee case.

STEVIE. What?

KATHY. You needn't think I'm hiding you in the wardrobe like Anne Frank.

STEVIE. But it might blow over, Kathy.

KATHY. So might the rain, but it'll still be back. (*Taking him by the arm.*) No, this time you're going, Stevie.

STEVIE. But where am I going?

KATHY. Don't worry, love, the easyJet has some great locations.

STEVIE. But… where, Kathy?

KATHY. Lenny and I'll take a weekend break to see you. Budapest! I've always fancied Budapest… or somewhere you can grow drugs freely – like Afghanistan! It'll be wonderful, you'll see.

KATHY *and* STEVIE *leave.*

Blackout.

SALAD DAY

Deirdre Kinahan

DEIRDRE KINAHAN

Deirdre Kinahan is currently under commission to Fishamble: The New Play Company, Dublin. She is co-writing her first feature film with the support of the Irish Film Board and working with Altered Image Films in London on her first television drama. She is also under commission to BBC Radio 4 for a new radio play. Deirdre's play *MOMENT* received its US premiere in Chicago in July 2012 and Canadian premiere at La Licorne, Montreal, in October. The Chicago run was extended and moved to a larger theatre due to popularity. She has two other plays in development. Writing for theatre includes *HALCYON DAYS* (Tall Tales/Solstice at Solstice Arts Centre and Dublin Theatre Festival, 2012); *Broken* (Fishamble, 2012); *66 Books* (Bush Theatre, 2011); *Where's My Seat* (Bush Theatre, 2011); *BOGBOY* (Tall Tales & Solstice Arts Centre at Irish Arts Centre/New York/Project Arts Centre); *MOMENT* (Tall Tales & Solstice Arts Centre/Project Arts Centre/Bush Theatre/national Irish tour); *Salad Day* (the short-play commission presented as part of The Fairer Sex series of readings on the Peacock stage in 2009); *Hue & Cry* (Bewley's Café Theatre & Tall Tales/ Glasgow/ Romania/ Bulgaria/Paris/ New York); *Melody* (Tall Tales/Glasgow/national tour); *Attaboy Mr Synge* (Civic Theatre/national tour); *Rum & Raisin* (Tall Tales & Nogin Theatre Company/national tour); *Summer Fruits* (Tall Tales/national tour); *Knocknashee* (Tall Tales & Civic Theatre/ national tour); *Passage* (Tall Tales/Civic Theatre); *Bé Carna* (Tall Tales/national tour/Edinburgh Fringe Festival). Theatre for children includes *Maisy Daly's Rainbow* (Tall Tales & Solstice); *Rebecca's Robin* (Bewley's Café Theatre); *Show Child*, *The Tale of the Blue Eyed Cat* (Livin Dred). Radio includes: *BOGBOY*.

Salad Day was first performed as a rehearsed reading as part of The Fairer Sex play-reading series for the Abbey Theatre, Dublin, in 2009. The cast was as follows:

PATRICIA	Rosaleen Linehan
SEAN	Des Cave
Director	Bairbre Ní Chaoimh

Salad Day was developed and rewritten as the full-length play *HALCYON DAYS*, which received its Irish premiere at Smock Alley Theatre as part of the Dublin Theatre Festival on 10 October 2012. It is also published by Nick Hern Books.

Characters

PATRICIA
SEAN

We are in the conservatory of a North Dublin nursing home.
SEAN, *an elderly silver-haired gentleman, sits downstage right,*
watching a flickering TV which is downstage left. PATRICIA,
an elderly lady, sits with handbag on her lap upstage centre,
facing the audience.

There is a handbag, keys and a cake box on a table, centre.

PATRICIA. She's a nice girl. Your niece.

SEAN. Yes.

PATRICIA. Stylish.

SEAN. Yes.

PATRICIA. I like her pedal pushers.

Hard to get away with them when all you're pushing is forty.

SEAN. Ahhhhh.

PATRICIA. But she has it.

Pause.

I think she put a lightener in her hair.

SEAN. Did she?

PATRICIA. Definitely.

SEAN. Ahhh.

PATRICIA. And you enjoy the visit.

He looks at her.

You enjoy the visit with your niece!

SEAN. I do.

PATRICIA. She's here, Sean.

She's gone with the nurse.

SEAN. Tom?

PATRICIA. No, Dee.

SEAN. Dee?

PATRICIA. Your niece. It's twelve o'clock, she's always on the dot isn't she I like that.

SEAN. Pat is always on the dot.

PATRICIA. Who's Pat?

SEAN. Dee's mother, like my mother. On the dot and lovely.

PATRICIA. Really.

Small laugh.

SEAN *laughs too, a little surprised.*

You're blessed.

SEAN. Yes.

Poor Pat. I believe she's gone.

PATRICIA. I think so.

But Dee comes.

SEAN. Yes.

Short pause.

PATRICIA. Has she the eclair with her I wonder?

SEAN. Hah?

She's gone to the table to check the box.

Oooh, and a cream slice!

Lovely.

Returns to her seat with the cream slice and starts to eat it.

SEAN *remains glued to the TV.*

PATRICIA. You're fond of an eclair, Sean?

SEAN. Hah?

PATRICIA. I said you're fond of an eclair!

SEAN. OOH yes.

PATRICIA. I've always enjoyed a pastry.

Not easy to find nowadays is it, a nice pastry?

SEAN. No.

PATRICIA. And nothing but sponge in this place.

Another pause.

(*As she eats.*) I think she'll be a while.

With the nurse.

SEAN. Oh.

PATRICIA. Explaining your new pills.

SEAN. Ahhh.

PATRICIA. It's their only conversation isn't it?

Pills.

SEAN. Yes yes.

PATRICIA. And do they make a difference?

SEAN. Hah?

PATRICIA. Exactly.

He goes back to the TV.

She continues with her pastry, then neatly folds the paper and stands to return it to the box, brushing the crumbs from her skirt.

She checks out the bag for the designer.

Very nice.

Then fingers the car keys and looks out the window.

Always parks in the same spot.

She returns to her seat.

Looks at SEAN *with intent.*

You drive, don't you, Sean?

SEAN. Drive?

PATRICIA. You drive a car?

SEAN. Ahhh had a Lambretta once.

PATRICIA. Yes

SEAN. Those were the days – travelled fast to Nenagh. Beautiful days.

PATRICIA. Ooooh Nenagh of course.

SEAN. Beautiful days.

PATRICIA. I'm sure. Like today.

SEAN. Today?

PATRICIA. Is a beautiful day.

SEAN. Is it?

PATRICIA. Oh yes. Just look out at the garden.

SEAN (*looks out*). It is bright.

PATRICIA. Isn't it.

SEAN. But you need to feel it.

PATRICIA. Yes.

SEAN. On your back. Through the jumper. Vrum-vrum. Glorious.

PATRICIA (*smiling*). Oh yes.

SEAN. Could hit at least thirty-five you know.

PATRICIA. Really. In a scooter?

SEAN. On it. On it.

PATRICIA. Oh of course.

SEAN. Then enjoy a bite at Egan's.

PATRICIA. Egan's, where's that?

SEAN. Portlaoise of course.

PATRICIA. Of course.

SEAN. And on you go… on a beautiful day.

PATRICIA. Oh yes.

And you had a car?

SEAN. I had a car.

PATRICIA. Oh excellent.

SEAN. Many a car.

PATRICIA. Excellent.

SEAN. Yes.

PATRICIA. And did you like it, Sean?

SEAN. What's that?

PATRICIA. Did you like your car?

He has tuned out.

Sean!

He looks back through the door.

SEAN. Is it Tom?

PATRICIA. No it's not Tom.

SEAN. Is it?

PATRICIA. No… no. It's just us.

SEAN. Oh.

PATRICIA. Having a chat.

SEAN. Oh.

PATRICIA. About Nenagh.

SEAN. Nenagh?

PATRICIA. Driving to Nenagh.

SEAN. Oh yes.

He looks again at the door.

PATRICIA *closes it.*

She sits.

PATRICIA. You see I never had a car, Sean. Well, I never had need for one.

Not in Rathfarnham.

SEAN. No.

PATRICIA. The school was only ten minutes from my door.

SEAN. Excellent.

PATRICIA. Yes.

Handy.

She smiles. He smiles.

I did have a bike when I was younger, so between that and the bus, I never had need.

SEAN. No.

PATRICIA. And I suppose I'm sorry now I never learned to drive. Yes, I think I'm sorry now, Sean, because it's more difficult to get around.

SEAN. It is.

PATRICIA. And I mean to get here!

Sure it's nowhere!

SEAN. No.

PATRICIA. You have to change bus.

SEAN. Ahhhh.

PATRICIA. Though Nora got a train for her last visit. My sister, Sean, she took the train and I said 'that's handy' but they're not frequent.

And that's the trouble, Sean, the train is not at all frequent to nowhere.

SEAN. No.

PATRICIA. No.

Pause.

Are you watching that?

Sean?

SEAN. Hah?

PATRICIA. Are you watching the programme. The television.

SEAN. Oh. No. No no.

PATRICIA. Nothing on it.

SEAN. Nothing.

PATRICIA. Absolutely nothing.

SEAN. No.

PATRICIA. But they keep them on.

SEAN. Ahh yes.

PATRICIA. They keep them on in every room, every day. Did
    you notice that?

SEAN. I did.

PATRICIA. And I've said it to staff. I've said 'why keep the
    blessed things on when there's absolutely nothing on it?'

SEAN. Yes.

PATRICIA. It's inane. I said that. 'Inane', a great word – and a
    waste.

SEAN. Yes.

PATRICIA. But then I think they're fond of waste.

SEAN. Do you?

PATRICIA. I mean you see the dinners; piled high! And I've
    said it to the cook, that one with the boots! 'It'd put you off,'
    I said.

SEAN. Yes.

PATRICIA. Puts me off, too much food.

Does it put you off, Sean?

SEAN. Yes.

PATRICIA. And the smell of eggs. I asked her that as well, 'why does everything smell of eggs?'

SEAN. Because we eat like birds.

PATRICIA. Who?

SEAN. Everyone.

PATRICIA. Well, that's because of the pile on our plates.

Puts you off.

SEAN. Yes.

PATRICIA. Of course.

Pause.

SEAN. But you get a good feed at Egan's.

PATRICIA. Do you. Do you, Sean?

SEAN. Oh yes.

And Davy Byrne's.

I like Davy's for the fine dine!

PATRICIA. Do you?

SEAN. Oh yes.

PATRICIA. Davy's in Nenagh?

SEAN. No, Duke Street.

PATRICIA. Oh yes, beside Marks.

SEAN. You get a good gammon steak.

PATRICIA. MMMMmmm.

SEAN. And a bottle of Guinness.

PATRICIA. Lovely!

SEAN. My favourite.

PATRICIA. Isn't that nice.

SEAN. Excellent.

PATRICIA. And do you miss Davy's?

SEAN. What?

PATRICIA. Do you miss it?

SEAN. What?

PATRICIA. Well, everything I suppose.

Life!

SEAN. Ahhhh.

Pause.

PATRICIA. I do.

SEAN. Yes.

Pause.

PATRICIA. Wouldn't it be nice to take a trip?

SEAN. A jaunt!

PATRICIA. Exactly.

On a day like today.

In a car.

SEAN. It would.

PATRICIA. Wouldn't it.

You could drive?

SEAN. I could.

PATRICIA. We could borrow a car.

SEAN. We could.

PATRICIA. I could just go home. Pop in – see Nora.

Explain.

You see I've haven't taken a turn in weeks.

SEAN. No no.

PATRICIA. And it's on the chart, she could see it.

Quite stable.

SEAN. Yes yes.

PATRICIA. So there is no reason for me to stay here.

SEAN. No.

PATRICIA. No reason at all.

Little pause.

And I could explain that to Dr Patten –

No strokes, no seizures, I'm fine – all this is a mistake… an unnecessary caution. Sean.

Sean!

He has drifted back to watching the TV.

Jesus. I really wish they wouldn't keep them on.

Pause.

But then there's no alternative in this place is there, Sean?

No alternative to the TV. Not here, no. No music, no bridge. I said it to Nora, not that she heard, deaf as a post and I'm the one they have in here! Nonsense, it's me that cared for her; me that performed the Heimlich when she persisted in eating steak; and me that kept her in drawers when she was suffering with the bladder and what's the thanks I get, what is the thanks, Sean? This. God help me, surrounded by wreckage. I mean you're the best of them. Now. And that's saying something! But at least you're a cultured man.

SEAN. Hah?

PATRICIA (*sighs*). There is no alternative here to television.

SEAN. Ahhh.

PATRICIA. That's what I'm saying, Sean.

SEAN. Ah yes.

PATRICIA. You think they'd put on a concert or something.

　You and I would enjoy a concert.

SEAN. Oh yes.

PATRICIA. Or theatre.

SEAN. Yes.

PATRICIA. The theatre, Sean!

SEAN. Yes.

PATRICIA. I've seen you many times.

SEAN. Have you?

PATRICIA. Yes. Oh yes.

SEAN. Excellent.

PATRICIA. Fluther Good.

　Willy Loman.

SEAN. Willy Loman…

PATRICIA. That was a sad one.

SEAN. 'A man way out there in the blue.'

PATRICIA. Hmmm?

SEAN. Yes.

PATRICIA. Well, I was – AM a great fan.

SEAN. Ahhhh.

　Lady Windermere!

PATRICIA. Oh yes yes.

She laughs.

A fan.

SEAN (*in performance mode*). And 'I wish I had known it, Lady Windermere. I would have covered the whole street with flowers for you to walk on... they... with flowers for you to walk on...' (*But he fogets the lines – tapers off.*)

PATRICIA. Ooooh!

Any more?

No.

Not to worry, Sean, you remembered all of Dan McGrew yesterday.

SEAN. Did I?

PATRICIA. Oh yes.

SEAN. Dangerous Dan McGrew.

PATRICIA (*in a bad yankee accent*). 'And the lady that's known as Lou.'

SEAN (*a little laugh*). Well!

PATRICIA. Yes

SEAN. A favourite party piece in Nenagh.

PATRICIA. I'm not surprised, it's marvellous.

And you made a nice change from the TV – you and Dan McGrew.

Pause.

It follows you, doesn't it, Sean, the theatre.

No reply.

Don't you miss it?

SEAN. What?

PATRICIA. The theatre.

SEAN. Ahhhh.

Pause.

PATRICIA. I miss it.

Pause.

I thought they might arrange a trip, from here, occasionally.

But no.

Those days are over.

Pause.

You see I used to arrange the trips for the active retirement. I was secretary.

I enjoyed that.

SEAN. Yes.

PATRICIA. I offered of course to do the same here but…
(*Sighs.*)

I don't know what we're paying for.

Pause

I told that nurse with the Italian shoes that you were an actor.

SEAN. Really?

PATRICIA. She was so surprised!

'Some of us had lives before here you know – we're not actually born in wheelchairs.'

SEAN. No.

PATRICIA. She smiled.

SEAN. Yes.

PATRICIA. She uses whitener.

SEAN. Oh!

PATRICIA. On her teeth.

SEAN. Ahhh.

PATRICIA. I think I took my first turn in the theatre.

Not a theatrical turn now, Sean – no – a stroke turn.

It was. Yes, at *The Vagina Monologues*.

SEAN. Really.

PATRICIA. Never got to the bottom of Mary McEvoy.

SEAN. Oh no.

PATRICIA. Had to be carried out through the auditorium.

Stretched.

My God, was it only then they started?!

Only January.

Seems like another life.

SEAN. Another life.

PATRICIA. Yes.

It came all of a sudden, Sean, you see, that stroke.

But then more – little strokes all the time – gnawing away at me, devouring me.

SEAN. Ahhhh.

PATRICIA. There's always the confusion first, hot, and then the pain.

Odd. Very odd feeling, Sean, to wake up then after and to be somewhere else and to not remember.

Sean!

SEAN. Yes.

PATRICIA. To not remember.

SEAN. No.

PATRICIA. No.

Pause.

And it's my liver you know – causing those strokes. Not my brain.

SEAN. No?

PATRICIA. So says Dr Patten – because I kept my brain sharp. Taught right up to sixty, then cards, crosswords – active retirement, active mind! That's the key you see that and peppermint tea… no dementia.

SEAN. Ahhh.

PATRICIA. You should have tried it.

SEAN. Yes.

PATRICIA. But then who ever knows what lies ahead?

I wasn't watching the liver.

SEAN. No.

PATRICIA. Sclerosis – despite the tablets.

Big pause.

SEAN *is back to the TV.*

Would you mind if I turned that off?

Would you, Sean, the TV?

SEAN. Oh. No. No. Not at all.

PATRICIA *puts her handbag down. Goes to the TV and turns it off.*

PATRICIA. Ahhhhh – that's so much better isn't it.

Pauses by the TV.

SEAN. Oh yes.

PATRICIA. A bit of peace.

SEAN. Yes.

PATRICIA. Before they're in on top of us.

SEAN. Yes.

PATRICIA. That's another thing.

The complete lack of privacy – I can't stand it. Noses around every corner – and I said it to that new manager – the one with the too-tight suit, but she paid no heed.

SEAN. No.

PATRICIA. None of them do.

I think I'll even slide this door.

She tugs at the patio door.

I will, I'll open it, Sean.

She opens it with difficulty.

There.

Oh my goodness, and it is. It is a beautiful day!

She puts her arm out.

Warm.

She puts her face out.

Oh, it's just lovely, Sean.

She stands at the door enjoying the sun.

Would you like to feel it?

Would you like to feel the day?

SEAN. I would.

PATRICIA. Well, come over so.

SEAN *gets up slowly.*

How are those legs?

SEAN. Good good.

PATRICIA. You sure?

SEAN (*stretching them*). Good ploughing legs.

PATRICIA. Excellent.

You need to keep them moving, Sean.

I've said it before, muscles seize!

SEAN. Ahh yes.

He has come to the window. He puts his hand out. Smiles. Puts his face out.

Warm.

PATRICIA. Isn't it.

SEAN. Beautiful… beautiful.

They both stand with their faces out the door and enjoy the sun.

A salad day.

PATRICIA. Oh yes. Of course.

A salad day.

Pause.

SEAN. It's a day for a swim.

PATRICIA. Isn't it.

SEAN. A day for Portmarnock.

PATRICIA. Ooh and that's not far.

SEAN. No.

PATRICIA. If we borrowed the car.

SEAN. Tom swims every morning.

PATRICIA. Does he indeed.

SEAN. Like a fish.

PATRICIA. Yes.

SEAN. I like to join him in June.

PATRICIA. Well, that's far more sensible.

SEAN. I can see him now in my mind's eye.

Out there in the blue.

PATRICIA. Well, why not take the trip?

SEAN. Trip?

PATRICIA. Today, Sean, why not take the trip today.

SEAN. Why not!

PATRICIA. Oh.

SEAN. And will you swim yourself?

PATRICIA. Oh no.

SEAN. No?

PATRICIA. Paddle.

I paddle.

SEAN. Ahhh.

PATRICIA. But I'm not one for sand.

SEAN. Oh.

PATRICIA. It gets in everything.

SEAN. It does.

PATRICIA. So if we're to paddle, we could do it in Rathfarnham?

SEAN. Rathfarnham?

PATRICIA. I used to take the infants to the Dodder for a tour.

SEAN. Did you!

PATRICIA. It's perfect for paddling.

SEAN. Really?

PATRICIA. Or I believe there's a pool in Terenure.

SEAN. Ahhhh.

PATRICIA. So I wonder. I wish… do you think you could drive me, Sean?

SEAN. Drive you?

PATRICIA. Drive me home.

SEAN. But of course.

PATRICIA. Oh.

SEAN. Of course.

PATRICIA. Really.

SEAN. Yes.

PATRICIA. And you think we'll manage.

SEAN. Why not?

PATRICIA. The legs are good?

He does a little dance.

With nervous laughter.

Oh right then – we'll just borrow these.

She takes the keys.

And we have the few bob.

SEAN. Excellent.

PATRICIA. And you'll be back in a jiff.

SEAN. No rush.

PATRICIA (*as she steers him out the door*). I could just point you back.

SEAN. Yes.

PATRICIA. From Rathfarnham.

SEAN. Perfect.

The door to the room swings open. PATRICIA *freezes, holding* SEAN.

PATRICIA. Hello!

SEAN. Is it Tom?

PATRICIA *goes to the door. Puts her head out. As she does,* SEAN *returns to his seat.*

PATRICIA (*to someone outside*). Yes yes.

Turns back.

Just the wretched girl with the tea.

SEAN. Lovely.

PATRICIA. No it's not lovely, Sean.

SEAN. No?

PATRICIA. No…

She returns the keys to the table.

I need to get home.

SEAN. Ahhh.

PATRICIA. To my own house.

SEAN. Yes.

PATRICIA. I don't want to die here.

SEAN. No.

PATRICIA. And I will die you see from the next stroke or the next.

SEAN. Yes.

PATRICIA. And not that I mind that, sure there's nothing left since they started.

But not here.

SEAN. No no.

PATRICIA. I don't belong out here.

SEAN. No.

PATRICIA. Do you?

SEAN. Ahhhhhh.

PATRICIA. Where do you belong, Sean?

Short pause.

SEAN. I belong with Tom.

PATRICIA. Oh yes. Tom.

I suppose it's different when you love someone.

SEAN. Yes.

PATRICIA. How lucky to love someone.

SEAN. Yes.

PATRICIA. I never did.

SEAN. No.

PATRICIA. Nora tried… more than once but…

SEAN. Ahhhh.

PATRICIA. I suppose it was always the two of us, since we were girls and – no room for another.

No reply.

Where is Tom?… Is he gone?

SEAN. No. No.

PATRICIA. But I've never seen him.

SEAN. No.

PATRICIA. Oh.

So he doesn't come.

No reply.

Well!

Maybe next week.

SEAN. Yes.

PATRICIA. Maybe.

For me.

And for Tom.

SEAN. Ahhhh.

He is back to TV.

She sits as at opening.

The NURSE *enters with tray of tea.*

The End.

NINETEEN NINETY-TWO

Lisa McGee

LISA McGEE

Lisa McGee is a theatre and television writer from Derry in Northern Ireland. Plays include *Jump*, *Girls and Dolls* and *The Heights*. Her short-play commission *Nineteen Ninety-Two* was presented as part of The Fairer Sex series of readings on the Peacock stage in 2009. She created the IFTA award-winning RTÉ television series *Raw* now in its fifth series, and is a contributing writer on the BAFTA-nominated *Being Human*. Other television credits include *The Things I Haven't Told You* and *The White Queen* (BBC). She is currently working a new sitcom for Channel 4.

Nineteen Ninety-Two was first performed as a rehearsed reading as part of The Fairer Sex play-reading series for the Abbey Theatre, Dublin, in 2009. The cast was as follows:

DAVID	Rory Keenan
JOHN PAUL	Paul Mallon
Director	Róisín McBrinn

Characters

DAVID, *twenty-seven*
JOHN PAUL, *twenty-three*

Two Northern Irish brothers.

Place

The middle of nowhere.

Year

2009.

*Lights come up on the living room of a run-down English
country house. It has obviously been abandoned for some time.
The room is practically empty. An old well-worn armchair
occupies one corner, a broken television is propped up on a
kitchen stool beside it. Downstage, DAVID sits at a cheap patio
table with a newspaper spread out in front of him. He struggles
with a crossword puzzle. The only item in decent condition, a
fairly large wooden strongbox, sits at the opposite end of the
room. JOHN PAUL sits on the box examining his bruised face
in a shaving mirror. His shirt is stained with his own blood. The
floor is covered with pieces of screwed-up newspapers. In the
centre of the room hangs a noose with a stack of books directly
underneath it.*

DAVID (*re: crossword*). Something – something – something –
E – something – something – S?

JOHN PAUL (*examining his face, wincing in pain*). Ah… it's
every time I open my mouth… I can… ah… I can hear a
crack… I can hear like a cracking sound… .

DAVID (*re: crossword*). 'This Greek daughter may oppose your
purpose?'

JOHN PAUL (*opens his mouth*). Can you hear that? Can you?
It's like a cracking sound.

DAVID. Greek daughter?

JOHN PAUL. Look at the state of me…

DAVID. Something – something – something…

JOHN PAUL. Look at the fucking state of me.

DAVID. E – something – something – S?

JOHN PAUL. Do you hear me?

DAVID. Something – something – something – E…

JOHN PAUL. Shut up.

DAVID *looks up from his crossword.*

DAVID. Or what?

JOHN PAUL. Or I – something – will – something – knock your fuck in – something.

DAVID. What's your problem?

JOHN PAUL. My face looks like I'm wearing it inside out. That's my problem.

DAVID. It was an accident.

JOHN PAUL. You should think about where your fist might land the next time you throw it.

DAVID. You got in my way… it was an accident… I hardly meant to hit you. What, you think I meant to hit you?

JOHN PAUL. I don't care if you meant to do it. The fact is, you did it. It's done.

DAVID. And all the crying in the world won't undo it so dry your eyes.

JOHN PAUL. You tore skin…

DAVID. No I did not…

JOHN PAUL. You did… look… you tore fucking skin – although to be fair that gyppo sovereign ring you insist on wearing did most of the damage .

DAVID. It's not a sovereign ring.

JOHN PAUL. It's still bleeding.

DAVID. It's a signature ring…

JOHN PAUL. And there's like… there's like a dent…

DAVID. It's called a signature ring…

JOHN PAUL. There… beneath my eye… you could have had my fucking eye out.

DAVID. Jesus Christ, how many times I didn't do it on purpose.

JOHN PAUL *approaches* DAVID.

JOHN PAUL. Feel it go…

DAVID. I will not…

JOHN PAUL. Go on… feel.

DAVID. I will not feel. Fuck off.

DAVID *returns to his crossword*.

JOHN PAUL. It's probably gonna scar you know…

DAVID. Probably.

JOHN PAUL (*shocked*). You think it's gonna scar! Jesus Christ!

DAVID. Relax, John Paul, I've done you a favour. It could only be an improvement.

JOHN PAUL. Everyone says I look just like you, David.

DAVID. Aye… after a stroke maybe.

JOHN PAUL. Fuck off, fuckwit.

DAVID. 'Fuck off, fuckwit'? I wish I had such an extensive vocabulary… this crossword would be a piece of piss…

JOHN PAUL. Will you just admit defeat and give up…

DAVID. That's the spirit.

JOHN PAUL. You're not gonna finish it, you've never finished one.

DAVID. That's not true…

JOHN PAUL. You're the same with them sudoku things… you just frustrate yourself… why do you even try?

DAVID. The same reason you continue to talk to women I imagine… there's a slight chance I might actually get somewhere.

JOHN PAUL (*dry*). That's good. That's brilliant…

DAVID. Do you know what though? You're right.

DAVID *turns the paper over.*

This is pointless.

DAVID *starts to read the paper.* JOHN PAUL *looks around the room. He goes to the window. He stares out.*

JOHN PAUL. The English countryside is a lot duller than the Irish countryside isn't it?

DAVID. Definitely. Do you know why?

JOHN PAUL. Is it something to do with rain?

DAVID. Partly, but mostly it's because you're a biased bastard.

JOHN PAUL *laughs slightly.*

JOHN PAUL. Yeah maybe. (*Beat.*) How did you come across this place anyway?

DAVID. That… that weekend I… that weekend I came over with the boys for Mickey's stag…

JOHN PAUL. Yeah…

DAVID. Well, after it happened… you know after I saw…

JOHN PAUL. After you saw her?

DAVID. Well, my head was just… you know…

JOHN PAUL (*sympathetic*). Of course it was.

DAVID. I needed to think so I got in the car Mickey hired and I just drove. I didn't even tell the lads I was going. I just got in the car and drove… suddenly I'm out here… looking at this place…

JOHN PAUL. I still can't believe you bought it.

DAVID. It had only been on the market for a matter of days you know. This old widower… he'd lived here for over fifty years… then the week before I pull up outside… he decides to drop. Fate.

JOHN PAUL. Fate?

DAVID. Fate.

JOHN PAUL. So what'll you do with it after... when it's...
(*Beat*.) What'll you do when it's over, you know when it's
finished... when it's done?

DAVID. Wait awhile then sell it I suppose.

JOHN PAUL. You will be waiting awhile.

DAVID. I don't give a shit.

JOHN PAUL. Like it's the middle of fucking nowhere...

DAVID. It's half an hour from Liverpool, JP.

JOHN PAUL. I can't believe you actually bought it.

DAVID (*annoyed*). We needed somewhere didn't we?

JOHN PAUL (*quietly*). Yeah.

DAVID. We couldn't exactly do this in a hotel room could we?

JOHN PAUL. No.

DAVID. We needed somewhere private.

A silence. The mood is tense.

JOHN PAUL (*lighter*). Well, it is that... It's private alright.
Nobody or nothing around... not as much as a fucking
sheep. (*Shudders*.) Thank Christ.

DAVID. I can't believe you're still afraid of sheep.

JOHN PAUL. Creepy wee fuckers.

DAVID. You should get hypnotherapy, John Paul...

JOHN PAUL. That's a pile of balls...

DAVID. It's not. Remember Mary Morgan?

JOHN PAUL. Mary from Derry?

DAVID. Mary from Derry aye. She was scared shitless of
clowns. She went and got hypnotised, she's totally fine
now... they don't bother her.

JOHN PAUL. Naw... I don't need to. Sure I'm never even around sheep...

DAVID. Well, Mary's not out drinking with Coco and Krusty every Friday night either, but it's an irrational fear. It should be dealt with.

JOHN PAUL. Well, I've coped so far.

DAVID *returns to his paper.*

A silence.

I'd like to have done this at home.

DAVID. Well, that's not possible.

JOHN PAUL. It would've been better at home.

DAVID. John Paul... come on...

JOHN PAUL. This is... I didn't want to say anything. I've been trying not to say anything but... it's playing on my nerves a bit now.

DAVID. I know. You're alright though. It's alright.

JOHN PAUL. It's this... it's just this waiting... it's just this hanging about...

DAVID. I'll make us a cup of tea...

JOHN PAUL. Good... yeah... I think I'm about ready for my seventy-fifth cup of tea ...

DAVID. What do you want me to do?

JOHN PAUL. I don't know make coffee... or hot chocolate or something... mix it up a bit... keep me on my toes.

DAVID. We don't have any hot chocolate...

JOHN PAUL. Jesus, my head's wrecked.

DAVID. And mine isn't?

JOHN PAUL. I know. I'm sorry. It's the waiting. I can't cope with it... the waiting.

DAVID *takes a bottle of water and fills the kettle on the table with it. He switches it on. He rattles around in a plastic bag.*

DAVID. Do you want a Hobnob?

JOHN PAUL. What?

DAVID. A Hobnob?

JOHN PAUL. I heard you. Where the fuck did you pull the Hobnobs from?

DAVID. I got them in that garage we stopped at…

JOHN PAUL. And why are they only surfacing now?

DAVID. I forgot about them…

JOHN PAUL. Forgot about them my hole… you were keeping them shy.

DAVID. I wasn't keeping them shy… if I was keeping them shy I wouldn't ask you if you wanted one.

JOHN PAUL. You're as fly as fuck.

DAVID. All I did was offer you a biscuit.

JOHN PAUL. Are they caramel or regular…

DAVID. Regular.

JOHN PAUL. Aye alright then.

The kettle boils. DAVID *begins to make the tea.*

Nothing changes. You would always hoard your sweets when we were weans.

DAVID. I was not hoarding the Hobnobs.

DAVID *finishes making the tea. He brings a cup to* JOHN PAUL. *He stops before reaching him, freezes and stares out the window.*

JOHN PAUL. Well, are you gonna give me it or warm your hands with it?

DAVID. I'm gonna fuck it round you…

JOHN PAUL. What?

DAVID. Which part of 'park the car around the back' confused you exactly?

JOHN PAUL. It's fine.

DAVID. It's not fine, John Paul… anybody could drive past… anybody could see…

JOHN PAUL. Nobody's gonna drive past. We might as well be up a mountain in a cave…

DAVID. Jesus but you're useless. We can't draw attention to us… to this. We can't draw attention to it.

DAVID *hands* JOHN PAUL *his tea.*

Here. I'll do it myself.

DAVID *lifts a set of car keys from the table. He walks towards the door.*

Useless fucking bastard.

DAVID *exits.* JOHN PAUL *now alone. Sips his tea. After a few moments a faint knocking sound can be heard, it's coming from inside the box.* JOHN PAUL *looks at the box. He puts his tea down and stares at it. After a few moments more* DAVID *re-enters.* DAVID *stares at* JOHN PAUL *who is completed fixated on the box.*

What is it?

JOHN PAUL. Knocking…

DAVID (*re: box*). From in there?

JOHN PAUL. Yeah.

They listen. Silence.

DAVID *returns to his chair at the patio table. He opens the paper again.*

DAVID. Open it up and check if you want.

JOHN PAUL. What, now?

DAVID. If you want?

JOHN PAUL. You don't want to?

DAVID. Are you afraid?

JOHN PAUL. Piss off.

DAVID. Open it then. Check.

> DAVID *reads his paper.* JOHN PAUL *cautiously opens the strongbox and stares inside. A few moments of silence pass.*

Well… has she come round?

JOHN PAUL. I dunno.

DAVID. What do you mean you don't know? Is she awake?

JOHN PAUL. I dunno.

DAVID. Are her eyes open?

JOHN PAUL. I can't tell… we… David, we…

DAVID. What?

JOHN PAUL. I think we fucked her face up pretty bad…

> DAVID *takes a sip of his tea, he turns a page of his paper.*

It's all swollen out… her head's huge now…

DAVID. She's not already dead is she?

JOHN PAUL. No she's breathing.

DAVID. Good.

JOHN PAUL. Let's just do it…

DAVID. No.

JOHN PAUL. Please… come on… please…

DAVID. I'm not finished.

JOHN PAUL. Let's just do it. Let's douse the bitch in petrol and spark her up.

DAVID. I'm not finished with her yet.

JOHN PAUL *starts to close the box but suddenly notices something else…*

JOHN PAUL. Did you… did you cut her hair off?

DAVID. Does that milk taste funny to you?

JOHN PAUL. Did you cut off her hair?

DAVID. I think it's out of date…

JOHN PAUL. You shouldn't have done that. Not without me. Why did you cut her hair off, David?

DAVID (*matter of fact*). She cut off his hair, do you remember?

JOHN PAUL. No.

DAVID. She did. He had long hair… do you remember?

JOHN PAUL. Yeah…

DAVID. Too long for a boy… he looked like a girl… do you remember? It embarrassed me back then. I would say to Mammy, 'He looks like a wee girl, people are gonna think he's a wee girl.' Do you remember?

JOHN PAUL. I remember. I remember his hair. I don't remember that she cut it off.

DAVID. She did.

JOHN PAUL. I don't remember ever hearing that.

DAVID. They maybe never told you because you were that bit younger, but she cut off his hair. Before she did it she cut off his fucking hair…

JOHN PAUL. I think… I'd like this to be over already. I'd like for us to do this now.

DAVID. I'm not finished with her yet. When I'm finished with her we won't have to do anything. When I'm finished with her she'll walk over to that rope herself, put it round her own neck and swing the way she should have done a long time ago. You'll see. Trust me.

JOHN PAUL *stares in the box again*. DAVID *returns to his paper*.

Close it again.

JOHN PAUL. I can't believe I'm this close to her... finally.

DAVID. I would fantasise about seeing her, and when I did I always imagined it would happen in some faraway place, some remote town in New Zealand or Australia... when really she was just across the water, she was in here in Liverpool. Six years in a detention centre...

JOHN PAUL (*correcting*). Six years in a fucking holiday camp.

DAVID. Six years then they slap her on the wrists... they say 'be a good girl... don't do it again'... and they let her start a new life within spitting distance of his fucking family...

JOHN PAUL. It's unbelievable.

DAVID. If it wasn't for that weekend we'd be none the wiser. The funny thing is I didn't want to go on Mickey's stag at all. I tried to cancel but the boys were having none of it. I wasn't really in the mood for it... or for them. I only walked into that bookshop to get away for them for five fucking minutes. (*Beat.*) And there she was... I knew right away... I mean she'd changed. I mean of course she'd changed, she was twelve then... She was only twelve then.

JOHN PAUL. And he was only three.

DAVID. Nineteen ninety-two... a long time ago I suppose... but I still fucking knew... I probably know her face better than she does, I was so scared I'd forget. I would study her photograph, I would stare at those newspaper cuttings until my vision blurred, do you remember?

JOHN PAUL. I do.

DAVID. Every feature, every flaw, every freckle... I knew. She hadn't a clue who I was. I bought this book from her... Ruth Rendell or P.D. James or... I don't know some fucking thing. I chucked it as soon as I got out of there. When I went to the counter with it I didn't speak. I was careful not to. I was afraid she might guess somehow… my accent or something, she's lost hers… .

JOHN PAUL. I know.

DAVID. Did you hear her speak?

JOHN PAUL. She cried out. She cried out for help… 'it wasn't me' she kept saying.

DAVID. She doesn't sound like she was ever Irish. That day in the shop she said… 'It's really good that one.' She was talking about the book… and she smiled at me… like she had the right to talk… like she had the right to smile… and when she gave me my change her hand touched mine and I had to… I had to get out of there quickly… I had to practically run out of there because I knew I was going to vomit and I did… I did. All over pavement… all over the pavement and all over myself.

JOHN PAUL. 'It wasn't me… It was somebody else.'

DAVID. I stayed in here for a week you know?

JOHN PAUL. 'That was somebody else.' She kept saying.

DAVID. I stayed in Liverpool. I stayed for a week after that. I watched her for a week before I told you. I watched her go to work… I watched her go for lunch… I followed her home… a whole week… and her life it's just… it seems normal… ordinary… like she's walking about pretending to be one of us…

JOHN PAUL. When she was calling out like… I started to doubt you, David. But then I realised what she meant… she meant that she wasn't that person any more, that she was different, that she was somebody else. (*Speaks into the box.*) It wasn't just him you know. That day you saw him in the park. That day he put his little trusting hand in yours. That day you led him away. Well, you didn't just take him… you took our mother, you took our poor fucking father, you ruined them, you ruined us. You don't get to be somebody else. You fucking animal. You evil fucking animal.

DAVID. Close it over.

JOHN PAUL *closes the box and sits on it. He picks up his tea again.*

Do you know what I always think about? When we were young… when he was alive and the three of us were children, Ma and Da would warn us about strangers, 'don't takes sweets, don't get into cars'… but the strangers were always men… bad men… we were all so busy watching out for bad men we forgot about bad women… we either forgot or we thought they didn't exist.

DAVID *turns back to his crossword again.* JOHN PAUL *takes a sip of his tea.*

JOHN PAUL. This is freezing…

DAVID (*quietly*). Something – something – something – E…

Fade to black.

End of play.

INVESTMENT POTENTIAL

Phillip McMahon

For Dee

PHILLIP McMAHON

Phillip McMahon's work at the Abbey Theatre includes *Alice in Funderland*, his first musical, which premiered on the Abbey stage in 2012. His short-play commission *Investment Potential* was presented part of the 20:Love series of readings on the Peacock stage in 2008. He is one half of pop-culture outfit THISISPOPBABY. As a theatre-maker he has worked as an actor, director, producer and playwright. His work as an actor at the Abbey Theatre includes *The Rivals*, *Translations* (2001) and *The Map Maker's Sorrow,* and he co-created and co-curated *WERK* Performance/Art/Club at the Peacock. His plays include *Danny and Chantelle (still here)*, *All Over Town*, *Pineapple* and *Elevator*. Directing credits include *In These Shoes?*, *All Dolled Up* and *A Woman In Progress,* all written and performed by Panti, *The Year of Magical Wanking* by Neil Watkins, and a live arena show for *The Rubberbandits* at Electric Picnic 2011. As a producer, Phillip co-commissioned and produced Mark O'Halloran's *Trade* for the Ulster Bank Dublin Theatre Festival 2011 (winner of Best New Play Irish Times Theatre Awards 2011). As an actor, Phillip has worked with many of the country's leading independent theatre companies, highlights include *Eeeugh!topia* (Randolf SD | The Company); *Under Ice* (RAW and Edinburgh Fringe) and *Jack Fell Down* (TEAM Theatre Company). Phillip is co-creator and co-curator of the *POP* performance venue (Electric Picnic) and *Queer Notions* cross-arts festival (Project Arts Centre). As a teenager Phillip was a member of Dublin Youth Theatre, National Youth Theatre and Australian Theatre for Young People. Phillip sits on the board of Project Arts Centre. He was Writer-in-Association at the Abbey Theatre 2009–2010.

Investment Potential was first performed as a rehearsed reading as part of the 20:Love play-reading series for the Abbey Theatre, Dublin, in 2008. The cast was as follows:

ANNE   Janet Moran
BRENDAN   Alan Howley

Director   Deirdre Molloy

Characters

ANNE, *twenty-nine, Brendan's girlfriend/wife*
BRENDAN, *twenty-nine, Anne's boyfriend/husband*

The action takes place in three different geographical locations.

Scene One

How It Is / Present

Dublin. An apartment. BRENDAN *sits in front of the TV. The apartment is furnished with new but standard apartment furniture.* ANNE *enters carrying shopping in Marks & Spencer bags. She's flustered. Throughout the scene she unpacks shopping.*

ANNE. They're pulling someone out of the river at Church Street.

BRENDAN. Yeah?

ANNE. A fella I think. Hard to tell really.

BRENDAN. Did he jump?

ANNE. Like I said, hard to tell, but I suppose he must've. It'd be hard to fall by accident. (*Smiles to herself.*) Some woman in Marks said I look like someone.

BRENDAN. Who?

ANNE. She stopped me and asked me if *I* was me. I asked her who she thought I was and she said she didn't know but that she'd seen me on *Dancing with the Stars*. I felt bad for her. She looked so excited. I said I was me, but I wasn't her off the telly.

BRENDAN. Stupid bitch.

Pause.

ANNE. Who?

BRENDAN. Your one.

ANNE. Ah no. She was just... I think she just wanted to talk to someone. She'd the small size of everything in her basket. Cooking for one I'd say.

BRENDAN. The Romanians knocked in just now.

ANNE. They've the music on full blast in there. The noise of them.

BRENDAN. It was him that called over; with a bottle of wine.

ANNE. Oh.

BRENDAN. They're moving. They've a van booked for the morning.

ANNE. Right. That's decent of them... everyone is moving.

BRENDAN. They're having a double celebration.

ANNE. Why's that?

BRENDAN. It's their Valentine's in Romania. They don't bother with ours.

ANNE. Like you so.

BRENDAN. Funny! It's called Dragobete according to your man.

ANNE. Were you stood talking all day or something?

BRENDAN. I'd no more interest of course. Full of the joys of spring he was. Probably gonna tear the hole off his missus. The day that's in it an' all.

ANNE. What did you do all day?

BRENDAN. Got sucked into Living TV. A lunchtime Jerry Springer reunited a redneck and his girlfriend who'd been cheating on him, and then they all got their gear off.

ANNE. Lovely.

BRENDAN. They *have* to be actors. There's no way...

ANNE. Was that it?

BRENDAN. No, they'd a black couple on who /

ANNE. Is that all you did?

BRENDAN. Oh. Yes. No. I checked my account. I can't afford to live here.

ANNE. I can afford it for both of us, I've told you.

BRENDAN. What does that make me?

ANNE. Grateful?

BRENDAN. I am.

Pause.

ANNE. I wish you'd go shopping once in a while. I could've done without Marks today. My feet are killing me.

BRENDAN. Ah but if I'd have gone then you wouldn't have got recognised!

ANNE. Huh?

BRENDAN. Your number-one fan. She wouldn't have spotted you.

ANNE. I'm serious, Brendan. I need you to help me sometimes.

BRENDAN. Alright. I will.

ANNE. Okay.

BRENDAN. Do you want some wine? Will I open that bottle?

ANNE. Is it from Romania?

BRENDAN. I'd say it's more than likely from Lidl.

She laughs.

ANNE. Just open it... I should really go in and say goodbye. I've never even said hello to that girl. I'm sure she's perfectly nice.

BRENDAN. Leave them to it.

ANNE. I went into Spar on my way up here. I have to say I hate the shop but it's closer than that new place. It's filthy, but it *is* closer. It's handy I suppose. I was having my stuff scanned when the gay behind the counter picks up my Flake and stares at it, then he stares at my tits, and then at the Flake again and he says, 'Are you sure you need this, love?' He's just looking at me, and I say, 'Sorry, what?' cos I'm genuinely confused, and he looks at my tits again, cos I've my coat open and I guess they're sticking out a bit. He looks and he says about the chocolate, 'We really don't need the business that badly,' meaning that I'm fat. Then he scans it and shouts, 'D'ya catch that, Lorna?' to a young one who *had* been stacking beans but was now in convulsions on the floor… laughing like. Then your man coughs, to get my attention, and as if nothing had happened he goes, 'That's €3.81 please.'

Slight pause.

BRENDAN. Why, what else did you get?

Pause.

ANNE. What?

BRENDAN. If it came to €3.81?

ANNE. Bread and milk.

BRENDAN. Why didn't you just get them in Marks?

ANNE. Because the arms were worn off me as it was. It's just handy to get the last bits downstairs. It's what I always do.

BRENDAN. Right.

ANNE. I'm not liked, Brendan.

BRENDAN. Would you stop.

ANNE. People don't say anything but I can feel it. I'm not well liked.

BRENDAN. You're too… here, have some wine.

He hands her a glass. She smells the contents.

ANNE. Is it muck?

BRENDAN. It's poison.

She laughs and tastes the wine.

You're too sensitive.

She considers this.

ANNE (*re: the wine*). I've had worse!

BRENDAN. I missed a call from Andy earlier.

ANNE. I spoke with Mags. Did you call him back?

BRENDAN. I couldn't be arsed.

ANNE. They've bought a cottage in Rialto. It needs some work she said, but they're gonna live in it and rent the other place out.

BRENDAN. Great. Good on them.

ANNE (*unsure*). Yeah.

BRENDAN. What?

ANNE. I'm just… it's stupid… I'm jealous. That's two houses, both alike in investment potential, and look at us… we're *still* renting.

BRENDAN. Yeah but those cottages are shoeboxes. And it's all about to go tits up anyway. It's any day now.

ANNE. Yeah but it's theirs. It's their bricks and mortar. It's the glue. It's the thing that'll keep them together, even if it's only for the sake of the mortgage.

Pause.

BRENDAN. That's depressing.

Pause.

ANNE. I'm fed up, Brendan. I walk home at night and I'm scared by every shadow I pass. I can feel this tension rising from the concrete. And I look around at all our friends and I wonder if we'll ever catch up. I hate myself for wanting what they have, and then I see this guy being fished from the river and I stop and wonder what it's like down there. And are we really any better off than he is?

BRENDAN (*surprised*). Anne. Come on.

ANNE. I'm scared, Brendan.

BRENDAN. Come here.

ANNE. What?

BREANDAN. Let's turn up *our* music, and drink our mucky Romanian wine, and just for tonight we'll pretend we're *them*, and if anyone knocks we'll pretend we're not here.

Scene Two

How It Started / Past

London. An old bookshop with books piled high, some new, some old. BRENDAN *reads behind the counter.* ANNE *enters. She browses for a moment.*

BRENDAN. Do you need some help?

ANNE (*smiles*). Depends… what kind of help?

BRENDAN (*laughs*). Er… I only know books. Not even actually. I only know the books in this shop… (*Whispers.*) and just the titles; I haven't read most of them!

ANNE. Right.

BRENDAN. But I bet I can find whatever it is you're looking for in the click of a button. I'm gifted like that.

ANNE. I'm just looking. Thanks anyway.

BRENDAN. No problem. (*Goes back to his book but remembers something.*) Oh… all the chick lit is down the front.

ANNE. Sorry?

BRENDAN. Your Maeve Binchys and your Cathy Kellys, you'll find them all to the left of the door on your way in. More hardcore stuff like Jackie Collins and Jilly Cooper you'll find alphabetically in fiction.

ANNE. Jilly Cooper?

BRENDAN. The horsey one. Dirty bitch too. (*Realises what he said.*) Oh sorry. You know the one though.

ANNE. I'll be fine, thanks.

She moves to a book stand. BRENDAN *watches her.*

BRENDAN. They're all on sale by the way.

ANNE. Okay.

She moves to another book stand.

BRENDAN. They're on special too.

ANNE. Right.

Pause.

BRENDAN. You're Irish.

ANNE (*laughs*). No shit.

BRENDAN. I'm Irish too.

ANNE. I got that.

Pause. She browses.

BRENDAN. I'm Brendan.

ANNE. Sorry?

BRENDAN. That's my name; Brendan.

ANNE. I'm just browsing, Brendan.

BRENDAN. No problem…?

ANNE. Anne.

BRENDAN. No problem, Anne. Take all the time you want. I'm here if you need me.

She moves off then comes back.

ANNE. Brendan. I do need your help, but it's embarrassing. I hardly know what I'm looking for.

BRENDAN. Try me.

ANNE. There's this book I've been looking for for ages. It's a self-help type of thing. It got great reviews. Nowhere seems to have it.

BRENDAN. Does it have a title?

ANNE. I'm not a hundred per cent sure. *Heal Your Heart*... I think that's what it's called. It's a bit obvious I know, but there you go. My face is burning now.

BRENDAN. Why?

ANNE. I'm mortified. The self-helpness of it all I suppose.

BRENDAN. You're fine. We get loads of crazies in here. I'm well used to it.

She laughs.

We don't have the book though. I buy everything that comes in and I've never heard of it. I can check if it's still in print though.

He moves to the computer and punches in some letters.

ANNE. I was at WHSmiths before, but they said to try here. Even a second-hand copy will do. (*Pause.*) What's with all the empty shelves?

BRENDAN. We're closing up. Everything is on sale.

ANNE. Closing? But why... this is a great little shop. I love it here.

BRENDAN. We've been bought out; compulsory purchase. We only own the lease anyway. Some old money-grabber owns the lot. In his seventies. He'll be lucky if he lives to cash the cheque... but there ye go.

Pause.

ANNE. I didn't mean to be rude before.

BRENDAN. Ha?

ANNE. When I... Where are you from back home?

BRENDAN. Oh. Dublin.

ANNE. Me too!

BRENDAN (*smiling*). Right! I study over here. Acting at Central.

ANNE. Me too... oh sorry not Central, but I'm here to study. I'm from Rathfarnham.

BRENDAN. And you're here to study.

ANNE. Maybe I'll stay. It's so expensive. I never know if I'm happy here.

BRENDAN. It's that kind of town alright.

Pause. They look at each other.

Your book doesn't exist I'm afraid.

ANNE. Really? Oh. I'll have to check again online. I must have the name wrong.

BRENDAN. Yeah.

ANNE. It's a shame about the shop.

BRENDAN. Nah, not really. It's just a bookshop.

ANNE. But it's yours. It's your bookshop. It's more than that.

BRENDAN. Nah, I just work here. It's my uncle's place.

ANNE. But still. It's more than that. It's a shame.

BRENDAN. I think the official word is progress.

She laughs, then stops.

ANNE. Well, you don't have what I'm looking for but /

BRENDAN. The shop.

ANNE. Ha?

BRENDAN. The shop doesn't have what you're looking for.

Pause, she looks at him.

ANNE. Right! The shop doesn't have what I'm looking for, but seeing as everything is on offer, I might have a look around and maybe pick something up.

BRENDAN. And do you need help?

ANNE. As I said… self-help. But as we've established, this closing-down shop can't help.

BRENDAN. But me. Can I help?

ANNE. I don't know…?

BRENDAN. Brendan!

ANNE. I doubt it, Brendan. (*Pause.*) I don't even know you.

BRENDAN. We had this man come into the shop last week. A big lad he was. Twenty stone at least. He had to move sideways between the shelves. It was… I felt sorry for him, but he seemed fine. I asked him if he needed help… the way you do, but he said he was okay. He didn't look okay. He was sweatin'! The man was stressed, so I gave him a few minutes and I asked him again if he wanted me to find something for him, a book like. He looked fully pissed off… cos his pride was all up in his face, ye know. But then he changes his tune, realising I suppose that I wasn't taking the piss, cos he must get that a lot, being fat an' all. And he lowers his voice, to that level that says 'we're speaking in confidence now' and he tells me about a show he watches on Sky that follows fat people. They all have personal trainers and nutritionists and all that. The results, he says, are amazing.

ANNE. Yeah?

BRENDAN. So at the end of the last episode they advertised a book based on the show, a spin-off kinda thing; 'Achieve this yourself at home'. Like, as if. So here he is, all twenty stone of him looking to buy this book to change his life. A book like. I actually felt like saying it to him. It's weird what some people will cling to. Like this is never gonna work for you!

Pause.

ANNE. Who?

BRENDAN. Your man.

ANNE. Oh.

BRENDAN. But I said nothing. You know the way.

ANNE. I better get going.

BRENDAN. Yeah. Sorry about your book.

ANNE. It's no hassle, really.

BRENDAN. If you leave your number I could try the lads in the
warehouse. See if they've ever heard of it.

ANNE. Yeah?

BRENDAN. They owe me a favour.

ANNE. Right. Yeah okay.

He hands her a pen. She scrawls her number.

BRENDAN. Friends in high places you see.

ANNE. Don't go to any hassle. Really.

BRENDAN. It's fine. You can pay me back.

ANNE. I best go.

BRENDAN. You owe me.

She leaves. She stops at the door.

ANNE. You have to find the book first.

Scene Three

How It Ended / Future

Las Vegas. A fancy hotel room, fifty floors high. There is a huge window that looks out across the city. ANNE sits on the end of the bed facing the audience. There's an open suitcase at her feet. BRENDAN fiddles with a champagne cork. They are on their honeymoon.

ANNE. There's suncream all over the case.

BRENDAN. What?

ANNE. I asked you if you'd wrapped the suncream.

BRENDAN. I thought you said packed… I'm sorry.

ANNE. I'll have to rinse some of this stuff.

BRENDAN. I don't know why we didn't just buy sunscreen here.

ANNE. I couldn't say no to Mam; she'd gone to Boots especially.

BRENDAN. Just have the hotel wash everything.

Pause.

ANNE. It's raining anyways.

BRENDAN. Ha?

ANNE. The rain… it's followed us.

He pops the cork on the champagne. He pours two glasses and hands her one.

BRENDAN. The guy who brought our bags up recognised me.

ANNE. What guy?

BRENDAN. The guy. The bellboy; he –

ANNE. But you brought our bags up?

BRENDAN. No – (*Looks at her strangely.*) some young fella carried them. Are you serious?

ANNE. I didn't see him.

BRENDAN. He shared the lift with us.

ANNE. And what did he say?

BRENDAN. Just as the doors were closing between us he said 'I know who you are.'

ANNE. Oh. Right.

BRENDAN. I'll check later what stations they get here. They might have some of ours on satellite. Either way…

ANNE. That's weird.

BRENDAN. Yeah it's mad.

ANNE. And had you said anything to him?

BRENDAN. Don't think so… Oh I said I'd no money for a tip.

ANNE (*realising*). Ah. Okay.

BRENDAN. What?

ANNE. Nothing. (*Pulling at his collar.*) Why are you still wearing that tie?

BRENDAN. It's how people know you've flown first-class.

ANNE. Is that right?

She removes his tie.

Is this too much? Should we have stayed closer to home? France maybe?

BRENDAN. Look out the window; Paris is on the doorstep… New York's out the back. We can even take a walk around the great pyramids! It's all here.

ANNE. It's all a bit… OTT.

BRENDAN. It's Vegas!

ANNE. I didn't think you got rain in the desert.

He pours more champagne, she moves to the window.

The smaller buildings look like coloured tiles on the bottom of a swimming pool.

BRENDAN. What?

ANNE. In the rain.

BRENDAN. Oh yeah.

BRENDAN *is changing his shirt.*

I read in the Aer Lingus magazine that a fella from Ballinrobe won a quarter of a million out here last month on one shot of a slot machine.

ANNE. Ballinrobe?

BRENDAN. Arsehole of Mayo.

ANNE. And how many shots had he had before that 'one shot'?

BRENDAN (*laughing, agreeing*). I suppose.

ANNE. Can we afford this?

BRENDAN. Of course.

ANNE. I shouldn't have given up work, Brendan.

BRENDAN. I can afford it for both of us. (*Pause.*) Anyway let's play the slots and win it all back.

Looking out the window, holding her champagne, ANNE *raises her hands above her head. Pause.* BRENDAN *notices her. He goes over where she is.*

What are you thinking about?

ANNE (*considers*). Nothing.

BRENDAN. Look at the lights all over this city. Imagine how much power it takes to make this place happen.

ANNE. And greed…

BRENDAN. Ah yes, greed. Of course greed; but commitment and power too.

ANNE. It's hard to believe we're…

BRENDAN. Married?

ANNE.…in the desert.

Pause. He kisses her neck.

BRENDAN. Did you pack your shoes?

ANNE. Of course… what are you on about?

BRENDAN. Your *special* shoes!

ANNE. Ah, my special shoes! I think you mean *your* special shoes!

BRENDAN. You don't like them?

ANNE. Yes I packed them.

BRENDAN. But you don't…

ANNE. I like them. I like how they look, how they make me walk when I'm naked, and I like what they do to you.

BRENDAN. But?

ANNE (*considers*). No but.

BRENDAN. And you packed them?

ANNE. Yes… have a look; they're covered in suncream!

BRENDAN (*smiling*). They're wipe-clean right?

ANNE. Right.

BRENDAN. Come on. Let's destroy this town. We'll get trashed and fuck like we did that first time.

ANNE. When? In London?

BRENDAN. In the store room… remember? My uncle was out front and I said I was bringing you out back to find some book you'd ordered.

ANNE (*smiles*). Oh yeah. And you pretended to look busy, when you knew all along that there was no book.

BRENDAN. No, there was no book.

ANNE. You were taking a chance. I could have reported you, or just walked out.

BRENDAN. But you didn't. You just stood there.

ANNE. So did you. You were probably thinking, 'Aye aye, this is a done deal.'

BRENDAN. I was holding my breath. I wasn't thinking anything. I was hoping.

ANNE. You looked sad. I touched your face. Remember? I told you it was okay. You lifted my skirt… do you remember? You didn't kiss me. Not that time.

BRENDAN. The door was slightly ajar because I had wanted to keep an eye on Joe on the shop floor, I knew he'd never follow me out back, but there are first times for everything.

ANNE. You're lying. You wanted the door open hoping that something would happen and someone would see.

BRENDAN. And?

ANNE. And something happened, but no one saw. I saw.

BRENDAN. That was enough for me.

ANNE. You put your hand over my mouth.

BRENDAN. To stop you screaming.

ANNE. Maybe.

BRENDAN. To stop you screaming. It was. I didn't care what Joe thought, but I wanted it to be between us. Just between us. And when I pushed inside you amongst all of those old decrepit books, it felt like the start and not the end.

ANNE. It was good. I'll give you that.

BRENDAN. We should be out celebrating.

She pours them both more champagne.

ANNE. Not tonight. I feel sick.

BRENDAN. Can I help?

ANNE. I don't think so, Brendan.

BRENDAN. Get some rest. It'll pass by morning.

ANNE. You should go out.

BRENDAN. Yeah?

ANNE. Do.

BRENDAN. I might check out the hotel bar. It's where Sinatra drank after every show!

ANNE (*smiles*). How do you know all this?

He holds up his glass to toast her. She raises her glass.

BRENDAN. 'Alcohol may be man's worst enemy, but the Bible says love your enemy.'

ANNE. Who's that?

BRENDAN. Sinatra.

ANNE. Right.

They clink glasses

BRENDAN. I'm going downstairs to drink some poison.

She lifts her glass.

ANNE. I'll finish mine here. (*Pause.*) When you come back I'll be wearing the shoes.

Pause. He stares at her.

BRENDAN. When I come back, I want you to pretend you're asleep... and I'll pretend you're a prostitute.

Finish.

RIBBONS

Elaine Murphy

ELAINE MURPHY

Elaine's debut play *Little Gem* premiered at the Dublin Fringe
Festival in 2008 where it picked up the Fishamble New Writing
and Best Actress Award, before transferring to the Traverse
Theatre during the Edinburgh Festival Fringe, the Bush Theatre,
London, and the Flea Theater, New York. In 2009 she was
awarded the BBC Northern Ireland Drama Award from the
Stewart Parker Trust, the Carol Tambor Best of Edinburgh
Award and a Zebbie from the Irish Playwrights and
Screenwriters Guild. Her short-play commission *Ribbons* was
presented as part of The Fairer Sex series of readings on the
Peacock stage in 2009. She is part of Six in the Attic, an Irish
Theatre Institute artist resource-sharing initiative, funded by the
Arts Council. Currently under commission with the Abbey
Theatre, they will be presenting the world premiere of her new
play *Shush* in June 2013.

Ribbons was first performed as a rehearsed reading as part of The Fairer Sex play-reading series for the Abbey Theatre, Dublin, in 2009. The cast was as follows:

LEWIS   Simon Boyle
GLENDA   Jane Brennan

Director   Wayne Jordan

Characters

GLENDA, *late forties*
LEWIS, *early twenties*

A small flat, old but meticulously kept. GLENDA *is waiting impatiently at the table, set for dinner for two. The buzzer sounds on the wall. She picks up the receiver.*

GLENDA. Come on up.

She presses the button to let her guest in. She checks her reflection in a mirror; readjusts her clothing and waits…

LEWIS, *an affable-looking guy, arrives. He is shocked by her appearance but is trying to keep cool.*

I wasn't sure you were coming.

LEWIS. Me neither.

GLENDA. You're looking great.

LEWIS. Thanks, you look…

GLENDA. Well?

LEWIS. Hmm…

GLENDA. Thanks.

Pause.

LEWIS (*simultaneous*). I eh –

GLENDA (*simultaneous*). I have –

LEWIS. Go on.

GLENDA. I was just going to say I have a bit of dinner on for you, it shouldn't be too long.

LEWIS. I didn't know we were having dinner; I can't hang around…

GLENDA. Oh right…

LEWIS. You didn't say dinner when we…

GLENDA. It's alright, I didn't, I thought you might hang around for a while.

LEWIS. No, I have to go…

GLENDA. Sure, I understand, busy lad.

LEWIS. Yeah.

GLENDA. You'll have a cup of tea at least?

LEWIS. Ah yeah.

GLENDA. Or a coffee, are you into coffee?

LEWIS. Tea is grand.

GLENDA. It's no trouble.

LEWIS. I prefer tea.

GLENDA. Me too.

GLENDA *organises the tea.*

LEWIS. Nice place.

GLENDA. It's grand.

LEWIS. You here long?

GLENDA. A couple of years. It was quiet until the students moved in next door. Thank God now they're gone for the summer – noisy bastards. I had a chat with herself, asked her to try for professionals or something this time. She said she'd be taking what she could get and hopefully we'd be lucky. Was the traffic bad?

LEWIS. Yeah brutal.

GLENDA. There you go.

LEWIS. Thanks.

LEWIS *organises his tea. Milk with three sugars.*

GLENDA. I'm surprised you have teeth. You should get one of those sugar substitutes, like Splenda or something, or herbal tea, or maybe one of those fruity ones for your sweet tooth.

LEWIS. Or I could just drink my tea in peace.

GLENDA. You could.

Pause.

How's your mam?

LEWIS. Keeping busy and before you ask, she still hates ye.

GLENDA. That's allowed.

Pause.

LEWIS. Is there something up?

GLENDA. What? No. Why do you say that?

LEWIS. It's like, well, you asked me here.

GLENDA. I wanted to see you.

LEWIS. That it?

GLENDA. That's it.

LEWIS. Just to talk, like?

GLENDA. Yeah, see how you're getting on.

LEWIS. Right.

GLENDA. So, have you any news for me?

LEWIS. No.

GLENDA. Not a thing happening in your life?

LEWIS. Not really no.

GLENDA. Something must have – are you still with that girl, what's her name?

LEWIS. Which one?

GLENDA. Ah what's this her name is, Susan or Samantha?

LEWIS. Sabrina?

GLENDA. Sabrina that's it.

LEWIS. We split up.

GLENDA. Ah, that's a shame.

LEWIS. When we were fifteen.

GLENDA. Really?

LEWIS. Yeah.

GLENDA. Oh right.

Pause.

How's your apprenticeship going, you're still doing that right?

LEWIS. I was let go there a few months back.

GLENDA. Cutbacks?

LEWIS. That and I was fleecing the place. They didn't know for definite. They had to make some cuts anyway it just allowed them to put my name to the top of the list.

GLENDA. A thief, Lewis?

LEWIS. Now, now, neither of us is in a position to judge are we? It's all good, I got another job there a few weeks ago; my labour hadn't even come through.

GLENDA. Have you ever been caught?

LEWIS. Once, by one of your old colleagues Garda Moran, I got off with a caution.

GLENDA. Of all the people, we hated each other.

LEWIS. He was alright; I think he felt sorry for me or something.

GLENDA. Where are you working now?

LEWIS. A warehouse in Santry Industrial Estate.

GLENDA. A warehouse.

LEWIS. It's grand.

GLENDA. Of course it is.

LEWIS. It's grand I said.

GLENDA. You know you can come to me about anything, don't you?

LEWIS. The way you came to me.

GLENDA. I'm just saying, my door's always open, always.

Pause.

You look different.

LEWIS. So do you.

GLENDA. Older. You're making me feel old.

LEWIS. You look old, even with all the slap.

GLENDA *ignores the comment.*

So what do you get up to all day?

GLENDA. Not a whole lot now.

LEWIS. No job or nothing?

GLENDA. I thought with time I could go back but it didn't really work out like that, ye know?

LEWIS. You could hardly go back on the beat you'd be battered.

GLENDA. I'll have to look into retraining or something…

LEWIS. You should apply to FAS, do one of them girly courses like beautician or hairdressing or something. You could practise on yourself.

GLENDA. Lewis.

LEWIS. What?

GLENDA. Go easy.

Pause.

LEWIS. Come on then, spit it out – I can tell by ye.

GLENDA. Can we not just have our cup of tea first?

LEWIS. So there is something.

GLENDA. I'm having an operation.

LEWIS. Is it serious?

GLENDA. It's quite a complicated procedure.

LEWIS. Are you looking for a kidney?

GLENDA. What, no –

LEWIS. – Or bone marrow cos I heard that's fucking sore an' all. I'll be keeping all my bits, alright, so don't even ask.

GLENDA. I'm not asking you for anything, other than a bit of support.

LEWIS. What is it then, are you sick?

GLENDA. Em I wouldn't say… no. No I'm not.

LEWIS. Hang on, is this for… it is isn't it?

GLENDA. I thought you should know.

LEWIS. Right.

GLENDA. Are you going to even hear me out?

LEWIS. We've little or no contact for five years and this is what I get?

GLENDA. You knew where I was.

LEWIS. And you knew where I was. Who's your doctor?

GLENDA. What do you want to know that for?

LEWIS. Because he should be struck off. The only thing that's wrong with you is that you're sick in the fucking head.

Pause.

GLENDA. I thought with you being that bit older you'd handle it better, that maybe we could talk about it.

LEWIS. You always loved the drama, didn't you? Well, no more. Do what you want; I couldn't give a fuck.

GLENDA. I don't believe that, I don't believe you'd be sitting here if you didn't give a fuck.

LEWIS. You've always done what you've wanted and you're dead right, it's your life, fuck the rest of us.

GLENDA. You think I'm putting myself through this for the drama, the last two fingers to your mother, is that it?

LEWIS. I don't know, Da, you tell me.

GLENDA. I've lost everything, my wife, family, career, most of my so-called friends. If I could've turned it off believe me I would've. But it's not going away, Lewis. It'll never go away. I have to do this.

LEWIS. So do it.

GLENDA. I'm scared.

LEWIS. Bet you fucking are. Who's going with you?

GLENDA. Sonia.

LEWIS. Is she a…

GLENDA. Yeah.

LEWIS. So she'll know what to do.

GLENDA. Other than hold my hand there's not a whole lot else she can do.

LEWIS. Where are you getting it done?

GLENDA. At the hospital.

LEWIS. You're hardly going the fucking Mater.

GLENDA. Thailand.

LEWIS. Makes sense I suppose with all them… how long are you going for?

GLENDA. Six weeks; I'm going to take an extended holiday, I'll need one.

LEWIS. Where are you getting that kind of money?

GLENDA. I got a loan.

LEWIS. With no job?

GLENDA. To be paid back when the sale of the house goes through.

LEWIS. You don't have a – our house? The house my ma and I are still living in?

GLENDA. She's looking into remortgaging.

LEWIS. You're fucking kidding me.

GLENDA. She has a good job, Lewis, and it's my house too, I'm entitled to half.

LEWIS. For fuck sake, you're unbelievable.

GLENDA. I've been hardly saving up my dole. It's the only asset I have.

LEWIS. Which your wife is still living in.

GLENDA. We would've had to deal with it sooner or later.

LEWIS. Well, at least the house prices are shit; I hope you get fuck-all for it.

GLENDA. I'm not interested in money; I just want enough to cover things.

LEWIS. Why did you even get married? I want to know.

GLENDA. We… we were great friends.

LEWIS. So you married her?

GLENDA. There's marriages built on a lot less.

LEWIS. It suited you.

GLENDA. It suited us. Your granddad wasn't the easiest man in the world… it's complicated; I don't expect you to understand.

LEWIS. Try me; you want me to be all adult about it, so let's talk, Pops.

GLENDA. We both needed a way out, so we got married.

LEWIS. How convenient.

GLENDA. And it worked for a while.

LEWIS. Until her clothes started going missing.

GLENDA. She knew.

LEWIS. Yeah right.

GLENDA. She thought I was having an affair at first, I think she would've preferred it if I was messing around.

LEWIS. What and she just ignored it?

GLENDA. As long as it didn't interfere with our family she was happy to go on.

LEWIS. So when you were caught in the club that night, she'd known for a while.

GLENDA. A couple of years by then. I wanted to come clean for so long but she kept begging me to put it off. I was supposed to be working that night; I got a swap at the last minute.

LEWIS. You must of nearly fucking died.

GLENDA. Yeah.

LEWIS. What was it you were singing again?

GLENDA. Ah, Lewis.

LEWIS. 'Chain Reaction'? You fucking tool, only you'd get caught by your whole fucking station.

GLENDA. I got home at some mad hour, totally locked out of my head. I woke your mother up and told her and she said: 'Well, you wanted everyone to know,' turned back over and went to sleep. I knew there'd be tough times ahead but I thought everyone would come round eventually. I mean my own wife accepted it but it didn't quite work out that way. It all just fell apart. You never came to see me in hospital. I could've done with a visit.

LEWIS. I got as far as the corridor. I was walking by some oulwan and she put her arms around me and started calling me 'Heathcliff', then she started bawling. I did a fucking u-ey and legged it.

GLENDA. I remember her; I think she just used it as an excuse to grope the youngfellas.

LEWIS. Mad bitch.

GLENDA. I didn't know you'd made it that far.

LEWIS. There you go now. That wasn't your first time in there was it?

GLENDA. I don't get you.

LEWIS. I saw you through the window you were calm, you knew the ropes.

GLENDA. It was probably the meds.

LEWIS. It was more than that, you looked... comfortable. Was it before you were married?

GLENDA. I was fourteen.

LEWIS. What happened?

GLENDA. Things were starting to change that I couldn't control. You have to understand I never felt like it belonged... I hated myself. It seemed like a solution at the time. I was so young, ye know?

LEWIS. What did ye... did you hurt yourself?

GLENDA. I cut it.

LEWIS. Your wrists?

GLENDA. My penis.

LEWIS. Ah, Da.

GLENDA. I watched the blood pour out of me and I swore that one day I'd be rid of it for good. Then I woke up in hospital, some poor surgeon had the job of sewing it all back together.

Your granny found me in the bathroom, insisted it was some freak accident but they knew. They sent this shrink fella down to talk to me. He was very nice. They kept me in for as long as they could but as soon as I was well enough I was marched right out of there. It was never mentioned again. After that any time I did anything effeminate I got a wallop. They didn't know what to do, either did I. How often do you do drugs?

LEWIS. What are you talking about?

GLENDA. Every month, every weekend, every day? What are you on?

LEWIS. '*What are you on?*' You make me sound like a junkie.

GLENDA. So you're not on drugs.

LEWIS. No. '*On drugs.*' I do a bit of this and that when we're out that's all. You know what it's like; they're all at it on your scene aren't they?

GLENDA. So it's not a problem then?

LEWIS. No, it's not a problem, for fuck sake. Did someone say it was a problem?

GLENDA. No they just said they were a bit worried about you. I thought we could nip it in the bud if it was becoming a problem, you know? I mean, you're still holding down your job and everything but these things can creep up on you.

LEWIS. What did you have in mind?

GLENDA. There's this place in Thailand, it's like a monk's place a monastery-type thing. They do chants and cleanse you and you do a bit of work for them while you're there; it's supposed to be brilliant.

LEWIS. Will they do a family discount?

GLENDA. I was thinking you could come over with me.

LEWIS. Ah you're grand.

GLENDA. I'll pay for it.

LEWIS. With what?

GLENDA. With whatever I have left.

LEWIS. The two of us can get fixed in Thailand what?

GLENDA. Think about it. It could be a fresh start for both of us.

LEWIS. Thanks for the offer but I just need to cut back on the partying for a while, stop enjoying myself so much.

Pause.

GLENDA. Sure you might as well hang on for your dinner now.

LEWIS. Honestly, no.

GLENDA. You could do with it; you used to be such a chubby little bugger.

LEWIS. It was puppy fat.

GLENDA. Puppy fat my arse. Are you sure?

LEWIS. Positive.

GLENDA. Another cup of tea then?

LEWIS. Nah, I'd better make a move.

GLENDA. Don't go yet.

LEWIS. I have to, it's this new job; they have me on mad shifts.

GLENDA. Right. Will I see you again before I go?

LEWIS. I probably won't get the chance… like with the new job as I said…

GLENDA. Mad shifts an' all. I get ye.

LEWIS. I hope it's worth it.

GLENDA. Me too.

LEWIS. Look after yourself.

GLENDA. I will. I might see you when I get back?

LEWIS. Yeah, maybe.

*She thinks about hugging him but he blocks her and they do
a kind of American thumb-gripping handshake instead.*

GLENDA. See ya, son.

LEWIS. See ya… then.

LEWIS *exits, leaving* GLENDA *sitting at the table.*

The End.

Other Titles in this Series

Howard Brenton
55 DAYS
ANNE BOLEYN
BERLIN BERTIE
FAUST – PARTS ONE & TWO *after* Goethe
IN EXTREMIS
NEVER SO GOOD
PAUL
THE RAGGED TROUSERED PHILANTHROPISTS *after* Tressell

Jez Butterworth
JERUSALEM
JEZ BUTTERWORTH PLAYS: ONE
MOJO
THE NIGHT HERON
PARLOUR SONG
THE RIVER
THE WINTERLING

Alexi Kaye Campbell
APOLOGIA
THE FAITH MACHINE
THE PRIDE

Caryl Churchill
BLUE HEART
CHURCHILL PLAYS: THREE
CHURCHILL PLAYS: FOUR
CHURCHILL: SHORTS
CLOUD NINE
DING DONG THE WICKED
A DREAM PLAY *after* Strindberg
DRUNK ENOUGH TO SAY I LOVE YOU?
FAR AWAY
HOTEL
ICECREAM
LIGHT SHINING IN BUCKINGHAMSHIRE
LOVE AND INFORMATION
MAD FOREST
A NUMBER
SEVEN JEWISH CHILDREN
THE SKRIKER
THIS IS A CHAIR
THYESTES *after* Seneca
TRAPS

Ariel Dorfman
DEATH AND THE MAIDEN
PURGATORIO
READER
THE RESISTANCE TRILOGY
WIDOWS

Stella Feehily
BANG BANG BANG
DREAMS OF VIOLENCE
DUCK
O GO MY MAN

Declan Feenan
ST PETERSBURG *and other plays*

Debbie Tucker Green
BORN BAD
DIRTY BUTTERFLY
RANDOM
STONING MARY
TRADE & GENERATIONS
TRUTH AND RECONCILIATION

Stacey Gregg
LAGAN
PERVE

Nancy Harris
NO ROMANCE
OUR NEW GIRL

Marie Jones
STONES IN HIS POCKETS & A NIGHT IN NOVEMBER

Deirdre Kinahan
HALCYON DAYS
MOMENT

Liz Lochhead
BLOOD AND ICE
DRACULA *after* Bram Stoker
EDUCATING AGNES ('The School for Wives') *after* Molière
GOOD THINGS
LIZ LOCHHEAD: FIVE PLAYS
MARY QUEEN OF SCOTS GOT HER HEAD CHOPPED OFF
MEDEA *after* Euripides
MISERYGUTS & TARTUFFE *after* Molière
PERFECT DAYS
THEBANS

Lisa McGee
GIRLS AND DOLLS

Conor McPherson
DUBLIN CAROL
McPHERSON PLAYS: ONE
McPHERSON PLAYS: TWO
PORT AUTHORITY
THE SEAFARER
SHINING CITY
THE VEIL
THE WEIR

Gary Mitchell
AS THE BEAST SLEEPS
THE FORCE OF CHANGE
LOYAL WOMEN
TEARING THE LOOM & IN A LITTLE WORLD OF OUR OWN
TRUST

Elaine Murphy
LITTLE GEM

Bruce Norris
CLYBOURNE PARK
THE PAIN AND THE ITCH
PURPLE HEART

Mark O'Rowe
FROM BOTH HIPS & THE ASPIDISTRA CODE
HOWIE THE ROOKIE
MADE IN CHINA
MARK O'ROWE PLAYS: ONE
TERMINUS

Morna Regan
THE HOUSE KEEPER
MIDDEN

Billy Roche
THE CAVALCADERS & AMPHIBIANS
LAY ME DOWN SOFTLY
ON SUCH AS WE
THE WEXFORD TRILOGY

Jack Thorne
2ND MAY 1997
BUNNY
MYDIDAE
STACY & FANNY AND FAGGOT
WHEN YOU CURE ME

Enda Walsh
BEDBOUND & MISTERMAN
DELIRIUM
DISCO PIGS & SUCKING DUBLIN
ENDA WALSH PLAYS: ONE
MISTERMAN
THE NEW ELECTRIC BALLROOM
ONCE
PENELOPE
THE SMALL THINGS
THE WALWORTH FARCE